My Maasai Name is Nemparnat

A Memoir of My First 3 Years in Kenya

By Heidi Totten

Dedication

To the Maasai, who called me home
Thank you for teaching me that the meaning of life is love, and
for introducing me to my Creator.

To my Family, who keep me anchored
Thank you for giving me wings to fly and roots to cling to.

Contents

Dear Reader,

What is the Power of 100 People, Working Together on Any Project in the World to Create Positive Change?

I am an accidental humanitarian. I didn't set out to do this kind of work, and I still wake up every day a little baffled that I get to do it. I'm just a mom from Utah, right?

I hope that you read this, and then share it with someone who needs to know that they can do that big dream that keeps them up at night.

This book includes some experiences that were very emotional and raw for me to go through. I have overcome many challenges, including losing friendships I thought would last the rest of my life. It took me a while to write this book, because I wanted to write from a place of healing, not open wounds.

I honor everyone who has been a part of my journey, especially those who were the most challenging. Those relationships helped me grow and expand my comfort zone the most.

If you are pulled to do humanitarian work, I am cheering you on. It is not for the faint of heart, as many of my friends doing this work will tell you. It takes a lot of patience and grit. Maybe a bit of pixie dust.

If you read it, and then it sits on your bookshelf or gets donated to a thrift store, it won't fulfill the purpose of writing it, which is this:

Anyone with any dream can achieve it. It doesn't matter who you are, or where you come from. If you have the desire to serve, make an impact, and help solve a problem in the world, it is possible. I'm proof of it.

So read this book, decide what you are supposed to receive from it, and then give it to the next person who comes to your mind. Stories are meant to be shared.

Asante sana,
Heidi

Safari to Your Soul by Denis Waitley

As you contemplate Creation
Wondering "why" and "who" you are;
And why life shines bright, but briefly
Like a cosmic falling star.

Bring your ponderings to Eden
To the place of mankind's birth;
Fuse the past into your presence
In the arms of Mother Earth.

Tell the lions of your struggles
Tell the elephants and birds;
Take communion here in silence
Midst the ever constant herds.

And relish in the knowledge
That "your being" fits this song;
That the harmony is real here
In this land where you belong.

Makes no difference your religion
For the Maestro welcomes all;
You'll be closer to your Savior
Than in any hallowed hall.

Hear the wind in the acacias
Whisper "welcome home dear friend;"
To the magic of beginnings
Where the story has no end.

When you're seeking self-fulfillment
In your urgent quest to win;
You can rest here, watch and listen
To the music deep within.

You'll find answers to your question
You'll release the unknown fears;
Of what happens in the future
Far beyond your mortal years.

Truth oft times evades us
No matter how hard someone tries;
It arrives by revelation
Standing right before our eyes.

I thought myself a wise man
But a novice to be sure;
Who has just begun his journey
Into love that's true and pure.

I'm a living, breathing instrument
One of billions on the stage;
Who plays his part with passion
With some notes on history's page.

Come with me to Kenya
Leave your masks and stuff behind;
Travel light with no agenda
Just an eager, open mind.

You'll discover in the vastness
Your connections to the whole;
And find inner peace and beauty
...On Safari to Your Soul

Foreward

Heidi Totten, or Nemparnat as we call her here in Kenya - that's her Maasai name, given and blessed by the community, is an outstanding woman with whom I've been lucky to work closely with for the past six years.

When she first arrived to Kenya it was just easy to notice the difference she had from the rest of the group. She had intention, she had cause and she had visions and missions to do here in Kenya. I remember the first time when she got sick and she could not go to the projects that we were doing and we came back after doing the projects and prayed for her and I could feel the spirit, I could feel her energy, I could feel the drive that she had in her.

The memoirs of Kenya as recorded in her book is a chance to see through her eyes the development, the challenges, and everything that we've been able to see growing in Kenya for the past six years. We've seen families transform, we have seen students graduate high school, we've seen students who we've worked with since they joined high school now working with us in the garden towers. We've seen an increase in the amount of Days for Girls kits we're delivering to schools, to orphanages, and to slums.

We've seen an increase from the garden boxes which we started to the numerous amount of garden towers that we are now doing in cooperation with USANA.

We've seen a number of families seeing their lives transformed through the income, through the students we've sponsored, now bring to the family, and have seen the whole growth in the organization. God has been so gracious to us. He's brought the right people to us. We have an amazing board and we also have the perfect leadership of Heidi Totten.

Through my own experience I've been lucky enough to be on the front row, the front seat, seeing all of these changes. I've seen her transform from the person she came here as, to the kind of leader that she has turned out to be. I hope that you enjoy reading and that we can continue creating more and changing more lives even in the years to come.

Moses Masoi
100 Humanitarians International
Executive Director - Kenya

Chapter One

September 2015
Out of the Inner Circle

"You're out of my inner circle!" I watched, somewhat detached and yet fascinated, as the woman who had been my mentor and friend for three years unleashed her rage on me. I put down my chocolate chip cookie. Suddenly, it wasn't as appealing. Tears were streaming down her face as she struggled to get control of her emotions.

I had been sitting in a back booth at Paradise Bakery with her for two hours, wondering when the tirade and ranting was going to end. Mentally exhausted, I had nothing to say in response. Her mind was made up, and if she couldn't control me, she would attempt to control who stayed friends with me. So be it.

It was just a few short months earlier that I had gone to Kenya with her, anticipating upon my return that I would go back many times, and that we would be able to work together. I was wrong. She told me that I would not go back to Kenya unless it was with her organization.

After six months of being berated over Facebook messenger, I was done. I didn't know what had happened to incite the anger, but I realized that if she had gotten to this point, we needed a long, if not permanent break from each other. I made the choice in that booth to move forward with what I felt was my calling in Kenya.

After a few minutes, I said I needed to go. In the parking lot I gave her a final hug and told her I loved her, knowing that it was going to be the end of the friendship. I was numb and confused, trying to make sense of what had happened that led our friendship down this path.

As I drove home, I thought of what all of this meant. Looking back, I realize I had no idea at the time the roller coaster of pain I would go through.

Part of me didn't believe that I would lose my friends, because really? These were adult women who could make their own decisions. I'm not one for confrontation and contention, and up to that point, I was the person who mostly went along with the crowd. Had I known what was coming, perhaps I would have made different decisions. At least I would have had different conversations to build bridges and make amends.

Instead, as the poem "The Road Not Taken" by M. Scott Peck says,

> Two roads diverged in a wood, and I—
> I took the one less traveled by,
> And that has made all the difference.

Chapter Two

November 2014
The Call to Kenya

I walked up to the door of the restaurant as a woman was walking out. She held the door for me and then said, "Hey! I think we are Facebook friends!"

That happens a lot in the networking world in Utah, which is very small. Everyone looks familiar.

"My name is Katie Jo," she said. I recognized the name right away. We hadn't met in person, but we had probably 687 mutual friends, so it was only a matter of time.

"Nice to meet you!" I said as I went inside the Wild Zucchini Grill.

A few weeks later, we both ended up at Bridget Cook-Burch's Inspired Writers Retreat at a cabin somewhere in the mountains. I felt an instant connection, and not just because we both happened to like Italian food. We were both there to write our stories, but looking back now, I didn't really have a story to write, yet.

After an intense couple of days of training, Bridget's daughter Bree talked Katie Jo into facilitating a drum circle to wrap up the retreat. I had never heard of a drum circle, and being a somewhat conservative Christian, I wondered what I was getting myself into.

There are moments in your life that are sliding doors. You get on the train, or in the elevator, and that takes you to one place, or you allow the doors to close, and that takes you to another. I briefly thought of bowing out of the drum circle, but curiosity was tugging at my heart, and besides, Katie Jo was cool. I figured if it got too weird I could always yawn and excuse myself.

Right before we started, our friend Heather shared a story about lions in Africa that she called **Run Toward the Roar**. At the time, Kenya was nowhere on my radar. Oh, I had a few friends who had gone a few times and took great pictures, but me going? Nope. I had zero desire to ever go to Africa. In fact, there were about 50 places lined up for me to visit and it would take a lifetime to accomplish that bucket list. Silly me. God had other plans, and He was about to push the big red button on them and set off a nuclear explosion in my life.

Run Toward the Roar

Most of us have seen a National Geographic or Discovery Channel special of lions hunting in the plains of Africa. What you may not know is that it's not the males but the females, the lionesses, that are actually the hunters. The males are inherently too slow and lazy. Sounds not unlike the human species!

The male does play a specific role, however. He will get on one side of a watering hole where gazelles or wildebeests have chosen to bathe. He will flare his mane, get as tall as he possibly can and let out a ferocious roar that would shake the nerves of any living creature within a 50 mile radius! The roar is supposed to scare the prey into running away. What the prey doesn't know is that the lionesses have strategically placed themselves on the opposite side of the watering hole. So when the wildebeest is running AWAY from the roar into what they think is safety, they are actually running straight into an ambush. If they had run TOWARD the roar, as counterintuitive and frightening as it may seem, they would actually be able to scamper away into safety. The male lion's "bark" is much more dangerous than his bite.

As the drum circle started, we took turns being in the center. It's hard to explain the intense energy of being in the middle of a circle with 20 people aiming drums at you. It's an incredible vibration, and when you think of how sound shifts water molecules, and then think about how our bodies are made up of mostly water, it's like all of your DNA is being shifted and rearranged in a 30-second period of time.

My friend, Becky Mackintosh, was the "anchor" for my circle, with Katie Jo, Travis Jessop, and another friend on the other three sides. North, South, East, and West. Becky set the beat, and suddenly, I was transported to the other side of the world, tall grass brushing my legs as I ran at full speed straight toward a row of male lions crouching in the savannah. They started to rise and their mouths opened in a roar as they saw me coming.

Just as I was ready to jump into the danger, the drumming stopped, and I collapsed into a pile of tears. The experience had released something, I knew not what, that had been bottled up for a very long time.

The next day I put down a deposit for my first trip to Kenya, which would happen six months later. The lions were waiting.

Moses, David and Me

Chapter Three

March 5 – 19, 2015
1st Expedition to Kenya

I opened my eyes, a bit confused as to where I was. Then I heard crowing roosters and a loud toilet flush and remembered I was in a tiny village in Western Kenya at a guest house called Eshemuli, previously run by Anglican nuns. Suddenly, I sat up as I realized, *the toilet had flushed*! Hallelujah!

For three days we had gone without electricity and running water. I was covered in mosquito bites, and had made friends with a gecko in the bathroom in my attempts to take a shower with lukewarm water from a yellow bucket. As someone who secretly hates camping (although my garage is full of camping equipment), I was struggling with the sleeping arrangements. The pillow was flat and hard. I was using my airplane pillow as a support in order to get rest. It was hot and muggy, as Kenya was in the middle of a heatwave.

"You can use the washroom, "my roommate said.

I jumped at the opportunity. Then, I took a shower, my relief washing over me along with the warm water. I got ready, putting on makeup to celebrate the occasion, and went to find the team for breakfast.

As challenging as the previous three days had been, I was in love with Kenya. The sounds, the smells, the smiles and waves from the children walking by the side of the road yelling, "Mzungu! Mzungu!" Nothing could have prepared me for the emotions that continued to hit me with each mud hut we visited, and each family we talked with.

The kindness and humility were something I had never experienced. I would learn this in depth later, but God was everywhere in Kenya, and I do mean everywhere.

The moment that blew open my heart happened the day after we had arrived in Western, the county where we began our humanitarian service. The compound where we were staying had a church, and as it happened to be Sunday, we decided to go and participate in the services.

It started at 9:00 am, which really means anywhere between 10:00 a.m. and noon Kenyan time. Nothing happens quickly, or on time. A member of our team went over to the electric keyboard and started playing. I vividly remember the church being swathed in purple.

The Church at Eshemuli

My phone was in hand, capturing pictures and videos that later would serve as a reminder of when the veil dropped, revealing the purpose that would drive me for the rest of my life. At the risk of sounding cheesy—it was a moment that took my breath away.

Throughout history, moments have been captured in one picture. For some people, that picture has gone on to become famous, shared in media and books all over the world. For others, it's personal, but life-altering all the same.

For me, it was the latter. A simple image that contained a smile that changed my world. As I brought my camera down, a veil dropped, and I saw everything about Kenya in a new light. It was if I KNEW the Kenyans we were with, instead of just meeting them for the first time. It felt like coming home.

A few minutes later, parishioners began filling the pews, and the deep rich sounds of African singing filled the air. I was still trying to wrap my head around what had just happened. Something had changed in me, but what?

After church, we headed to visit families. As a team, we had fundraised for goats and cows to donate to these families, and we wanted to visit and get to know them.

I had not been prepared for what I was seeing, as we walked down the dusty road lined with a variety of trees and bushes that were slightly shriveled from a delay of the short rainy season.

There was so much to look at, and I was trying to take it all in. My heart filled with gratitude that my friends had convinced me to come.

Along a road in Western Kenya

Children ran alongside us giggling and asking for sweets. I stopped and took a selfie with them, and they gathered around me to look at the result, crowding to look at the screen, and bursting into fresh giggles after seeing their faces.

My mind was experiencing cognitive dissonance. Weren't they supposed to be poor starving Africans? Why were they so happy? Why were they so much happier than children at home? What in the world was happening to me?

"They don't need us, do they?" I remember asking one of my team members who had been to Kenya before.

"No, they really don't. We need them," was her reply.

I had a lot to learn about a lot of things, and it was just the beginning. So much felt out of place, or perhaps so much was falling into place. Our days were so full it was hard to process anything before falling into bed exhausted.

In the evenings at the guest house, we would sit around and talk after dinner under the thatched roof of the pavilion where our meals were served. I had so many questions, and felt awkward asking them. Instead, I listened to the stories.

Our team consisted of eight American women and six Kenyans. Suchi was the director in Western Kenya, leading us on projects and workshops. Christine was a shy and reserved woman from Nairobi, who owned a sewing shop. Dominic was a funny and talkative man from Kisii, who kept us all laughing. Moses and David were Maasai warriors, who would later lead us on safari, and Godfrey was our driver.

Since I typically get carsick, I mostly hung out in the front seat with Godfrey, listening to Christian rock and talking about life. We became good friends over those few days he drove us around in a rattling old van. A day in Kenya feels like a week in the United States. Time works differently there.

After two days of visiting families and teaching a goal-setting workshop in the heat, my body was done. I needed a break. The team was heading out to plant trees and visit an orphanage, so I decided to stay back to rest, do laundry, and write in my journal.

It was one of my best days. I had made a playlist of music for the trip, and spent most of the day listening to it and napping. Later in the afternoon I ventured out to the compound to write under the pavilion, when a man named Francis who worked at the guest house came to talk with me. He shared with me his dream of starting a small shop, and after a few minutes said, "Wait, I need to get some paper. I want to write down what you tell me to do."

"Why a small shop?" I asked him. "Why not a medium-sized shop?"

His eyes got big at the possibility. It seemed so simple to me, but as I explained it, he caught the vision. In exchange, he taught me some words in Swahili. They are written inside the cover of that journal in his handwriting. Sometimes I think about Francis and whether or not he started that shop. Knowing what I know about Kenya, it's not likely that he did, but I can hope.

I'm not sure if I helped him or hurt him by painting that picture in his mind of what I thought was possible. I've learned since then that I have to be more careful. But Francis gave me a gift that day, and I got a glimpse of the mindset of poverty, and the hesitancy to dream big. It was a valuable lesson.

When the team returned after dark, Dominic and Christine came into my room and sat down and prayed with me that I would feel better and that my body would heal. Their faith made me stronger, and I would definitely need it later.

Faith. That was one thing that kept coming to mind. I was experiencing faith on a completely new level.

Even now, it's so hard to put into words what I experienced those first few days in Western Kenya. I was covered in mosquito bites, hadn't had a shower, and if we hadn't brought a ton of snacks, I probably wouldn't have eaten, and yet each day I would text my husband and tell him I couldn't wait to come back and bring him.

Later that night, as I listened to Moses and David sing quietly, I felt incredible gratitude. Not for what I had at home, but for seeing what people live without. I will never forget those first few days spent in the jungles of Western Kenya. If I close my eyes I can hear the monkeys and smell the campfires. I can feel the heat of the sun, so close to the equator that we crossed it on the road. The sound of the African drums beats in my heart and heals my soul.

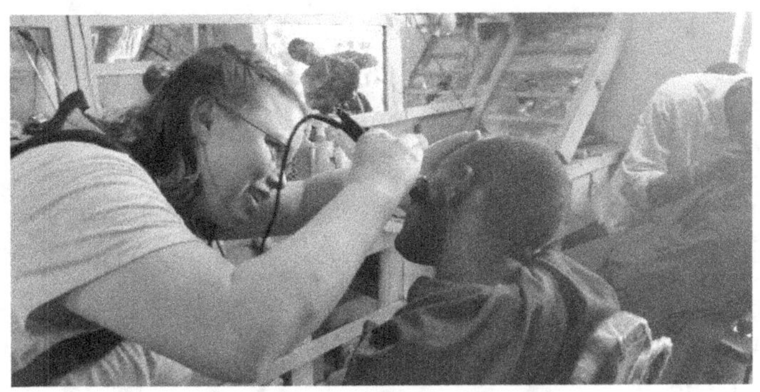

Shaving David at the Barber Shop

One of my most liked pictures on Facebook from that trip was one of me shaving David in a barber shop along the road. We were driving home when suddenly Godfrey pulled over by the side of the road. Kenyans are notorious for doing this and not explaining to Americans what is happening. Since the plans were discussed in Swahili, he assumed that I knew what was going on.

We piled out of the van and a few of the team went to check out the fresh fruit being sold at the market. The rest of us followed the Maasai to the barber shop; they needed a shave. I mean, why not, right?

I remember my friend Jason Hewlett commented and said, "You won the internet today."

A few of us took turns shaving David, who at the time was pretty quiet, but I wouldn't say that about him now. His English has improved a great deal over the years.

"When you woke up this morning, did you think that four American women would take turns shaving you this afternoon?" I asked him.

"No. Really, no." he replied.

Funny things happen like this in Kenya. Now, I'm used to it. Back then, everything was a novelty. They must have gotten sick of me commenting on so many things, but they never let on that they were. Perhaps they were used to Americans asking questions. Over the years, shaving David became a regular thing. Stopping suddenly to do something without any notice became a regular thing. When I take teams to Kenya, the questions come to me now.

"What are we doing?" they ask.

"I don't know, " is usually my response. Because I don't.

I'm also used to random Kenyans jumping in and out of vans, cars, and jeeps en route to somewhere else. I rarely plan to see people I know outside of my Kenyan team, but I usually end up seeing most of them throughout a trip.

One time we dropped our friend Sammy off at The Galleria Mall in Nairobi, right before we headed to the airport. On the next trip, we stopped at The Galleria Mall on our way to our hotel from the airport after arriving. Sammy walked up to my window to say hi. It had been six months.

Did he live at the mall? No idea. To this day I usually see Sammy at that mall. He drives by and sees our jeeps and stops in to say hello. I've just gotten used to the surprises. Kenyans have a crazy way of communication and networking that is nowhere to be found in the U.S. To be honest, it's way more efficient. Okay, back to the story.

Our last night at Eshemuli, I stayed up way too late talking to Dominic and Moses. We were scheduled to leave at 4:00 a.m. to travel five hours to Kisii, and it was around 2:00 a.m. when our conversation wrapped up and I went to bed. It was my first opportunity to just spend time with members of the Kenyan team with no one else around.

Dominic and Moses are tour guides, and hospitality is huge in Kenya. It takes a while to break through host formality and create real friendships. Even Christine tells a part of her story in which I was bugging her and she just wanted me to go away. I was pretty determined to get to know them, and not just have surface conversations with them. I just remember feeling it was really important that I wasn't just another visitor.

Dominic is a talker. Moses is not. So in that conversation I heard Dominic's life story, while Moses listened, probably wondering when I was going to leave so that he could sleep. I think I finally left around 2:00 am when my eyes would no longer stay open.

Morning came about two hours later, and we all rolled out of bed, only to sit and wait for another hour before the vans arrived. We did the best we could to sleep in the van, but the seats were incredibly uncomfortable, and we were surrounded by luggage threatening to pummel us.

We arrived in Kisii at a school to a great deal of fanfare, including dancing, singing, and a drunk trumpet player serenading us continually. It was definitely a different vibe and feeling from Western Kenya. There are 44 tribes, and each one I have worked with has a unique culture. There's very little crossover in the villages.

The school administrators brought us into their office and fed us popcorn and soda. They shared with us the challenges they were facing. One woman in particular became very passionate about something called FGM. I had never heard of it, but it sounded as though it was a huge problem in their community.

Later, I learned that it stood for Female Genital Mutilation, or Female Circumcision. They estimated that 98% of girls in Kisii had experienced it.

The feeling that came over me when I understood what it was is indescribable. There are a few tribes who practice it still in Kenya, even though it is illegal. Another thing to process. It was a very dark and heavy moment on the trip.

Our team was there to do a goal-setting workshop for the students. It was a disaster. We were outside under a tent, and it was incredibly hot and humid. The students sitting in the front row were completely stoned with bloodshot eyes. We were tired and had zero energy, and everything had to be translated into English. We finally finished, and just then the heavens opened up and it began to rain. I think I cried. I know I danced!

After an afternoon nap, we headed up Mt. Kisii where we took team pictures with the sunset. Kisii is a beautiful town with mountains and green tea plantations. It was settled by the British and centers around agriculture. It's also well-known for soapstone, which is a popular souvenir for tourists. I have gathered a lot of it over the years.

David, Dominic, Moses and Me in Kisii

We stayed the night in Kisii, where we were greeted the next day with a horrible pink cake for breakfast. I'm not kidding. It was huge and cinnamon flavored. And very pink. The hotel wanted to thank our team for coming. There was a whole strange ceremony around cutting that cake. I've learned that Kenyans take cake-cutting very seriously, and unfortunately, it's a pretty frequent event when I'm there. Let's just say that was the worst cake I have ever had in my life.

After driving for a few hours, we arrived in Narok, the closest town to the Maasai Mara, which is currently the #1 safari destination in the world. We stopped at the Narok Coffee Shop where I met Moses's wife and six-month old daughter, Shantel. I was in love. I'm still in love. That was March 13, 2015.

That day, I went home for the first time when we turned on the road to the Mara.

But first, it was time for a safari!

Safari should be on everyone's bucket list. It's the only experience for which Kenyans arrive on time. If they tell you to be ready for safari at 6:00 a.m., they mean it. If they tell you to be ready for anything else at 9:00 a.m., you should be almost ready at 10:00 a.m.

Our first morning on the Mara, we were up before the sun and heading to the savannah. It was cold, but we knew that once the sun came up we would be roasting. As we headed through the gate, we were greeted by zebra, after zebra, after zebra. We kept yelling at the drivers to stop so we could take pictures, until finally Moses said, "If we stop for every zebra, we are going to see nothing but zebras." We kept going.

A few minutes later, we came around the corner upon two cheetahs dozing under a bush. Since I had wanted to see cheetahs more than anything else, I was really excited. My daughter at the time was nine years old and just wanted cheetah pictures. Right then, I mentally wrote on my bucket list to someday pet a cheetah. The odds weren't in my favor.

Cheetahs on Safari

We saw a lot of animals that day, including four of the Big Five, which include the lion, leopard, elephant, cape buffalo, and rhino. The only thing missing was a rhino, but we still had another full day on safari to find one.

I ended the day with a sunburn, and bruises all over my side from standing up in the jeep and hitting my ribs on the metal bars. But it was worth it. Did I mention the sunburn?

The next day was Sunday, so we headed to church to meet Moses's mom. One of the nights in Western Kenya, Moses had shared his mom's story about bringing Christianity to that area of the Mara, so my mind had built her into quite the legend.

Mama Helen is a fun and funny force to be reckoned with. As I have gotten to know her over the years, we have developed our own language – a mix of Swahili, English, and a little bit of Maasai from time to time. When Mama Helen prays, God listens. And acts. That woman has faith that moves mountains.

In the afternoon, we hosted a workshop at our friend JJ's church, where I remember saying something dumb. Moses stepped in and covered for me. Seriously, I'm so unbelievably awkward in Kenya, but they seem to tolerate my quirks.

In sharing all of this, I am introducing you to the people in Kenya who impacted me the most on that first trip. They are the reason I had to go back.

I mean, did they really care if I returned? I don't know. For a while I wondered, and then it didn't matter. As I said, I needed Kenya far more than Kenya needed me. The country and its people have molded me and transformed me into a different person. They are my refiner's fire.

Our final night on the Mara was to be spent in a mud hut at a cultural village way up in the hills. But first, we spent the day as a Maasai. This was the moment I had been most excited about, even though I didn't really know much about the Maasai before going to Kenya. Turns out many people have heard of the Maasai, but since I had never intended to go to Africa—EVER—it wasn't on my radar.

The village we visited was in an area called Nkoilale. We were greeted by the "Wall of Warriors" singing and dancing for us in a welcome, and then watched the amazing Maasai jumping competition. The warrior who jumps the highest chooses the most girlfriends. True story.

Our next adventure led us into the village to learn how the Maasai live. The huts were small, cramped, dark, and mostly full of smoke. We all had to turn on our cell phone flashlights to see anything. The Maasai cook their meals inside to warm the huts, called manyattas, and to keep the mosquitos at bay. There are tiny windows that let in almost no light, but Maasai have incredible vision and can see in the dark.

We gathered outside of the huts to receive our Maasai names and a blessing from an elder.

At this point I really had no idea of what God's plan was for me in Kenya. I mean, I knew that I would return, but when and how often was unknown to me. I'm grateful that the choosing of my name was caught on video, because it was at the time so insignificant, and yet, incredibly important, which you will understand if you manage to stick with me through this story.

My Maasai name is Nemparnat.

There are much prettier sounding names in the Maasai language, but mine is perfect.

JJ Explaining my Maasai Name

As we headed to our last night on the Mara, I reflected on the day and my experience. I had no words to describe what I had felt, being among the Maasai, but it was a knowing deep in my soul that something had begun.

Not everyone has that experience with them. I think the Maasai choose people, but they might laugh at me for saying that.

We arrived at the village in the darkness, once again lighting the night with our cell phone flashlights. There were no other lights, and the stars were everywhere.

After slaughtering a goat, an experience that drove me to run around a hut and hide with my hands over my ears, we settled in to eat dinner and visit.

We sat in plastic chairs, and it turned into a makeshift salon as the children ran their dirty, dusty fingers through our hair. We didn't care. Turns out that dust makes a great volumizer.

Around midnight, Moses stood up and asked us to share what we loved about Kenya. When he got to me, I started sobbing. Not crying. No, there was nothing dignified about it. This was hysterical, gulping, snotfilled, ridiculous gasps of air just trying to talk. And I couldn't say a word. I just kept making that sound.

Moses moved on, periodically coming back to me to see if I had composed myself. At the very end, I hiccupped and lurched my way through…something. I mean, I don't have any idea what I said, and I'm certain no one else understood it, either.

Maasai don't cry.

I went to sleep that night with my headlamp on to make sure I saw the spiders before they ate me. I was sick to my stomach, having taken an antibiotic on very little food (because I couldn't eat the goat). Fortunately, Heather, who will forever be an angel in my life, gave me her very last protein bar.

It was the worst night of sleep of my life. As much as I love the Maasai, it's probably a good thing for them that I don't try very hard to live like they do when I'm in Kenya.

It had been a long, dry, and dusty day, and after a few hours, we woke up in the dark to a full day game drive where we saw a rhino. The Big Five completed.

As I said goodbye at the Keekorok Airstrip to David, he grabbed my cheeks and said, "Promise me. Promise me you will come back."

I promised.

I cried the entire flight to Nairobi. We finally arrived at our hotel and I remember saying to Tina, "I smell like everything." After a hot shower and pizza, I slept for the first time in two days. We were back in the "real" world. The final day we visited the Kazuri Bead Factory and ate lunch at The Galleria before heading to the airport.

And that was my first trip to Kenya.

I came home, super excited to see what I could do further, not realizing that my intense love of the land and the people would radically change my life. I had no idea that I would have to choose these people that I barely knew over my core group of friends. I had no clue that I would spend the next eight weeks crying every time anyone asked me about my trip.

Looking back, would I have changed anything? No. I have often expressed to Moses, Christine, and David that I would do it all over, and I would.

Nemparnat means (loosely translated) a wise person who gathers people to a permanent home.

Do you want to go to Kenya?

Chapter Four

June 2015
"Healer Week"

It was around eight weeks after I got home from my first trip to Kenya that I stopped crying and started planning. The last two weeks of the month included some sort of healing/retreat/ workshop/therapy opportunity, so I booked out a few massages and energy sessions and called it "Healer Week." I figured on the other side of that experience was some sort of direction.

It kicked off with a two-and-a-half-day event called Ignite that my friend Angella was hosting. Angella had been in Kenya with us, and our two other friends Heather and Tina were there as well. Just being with them was therapeutic.

It was at that event that I learned to ask the question, "What else is possible?" It opened up all sorts of ideas for me about the projects I could work on in with families in Kenya.

One of the Kenya projects I was interested in helping with was getting our friend Christine to Uganda to go through Days for Girls University. It wasn't my idea, but a mutual friend brought it to me and asked if I would help raise the funds. I asked Angella if she would be willing to fundraise during Ignite, and we were able to quickly raise the $1600 needed.

Later, that proved to be a big deal for my organization and what we do for our Women's Initiatives. Days for Girls provides reusable feminine hygiene kits to girls around the world. What we were able to help Christine start was an enterprise in which she would be able to enlist her sewing team in helping make the kits. She trains girls all over Kenya in workshops, and on every expedition we have been able to have Christine join us as we have raised the funds for kits.

Each kit is $10, which keeps a girl in school for up to three years instead of missing due to her period. The kit pays for the materials, as well as providing an income to the women who sew them. They can use it to support their families. That program became the first major pillar for our expeditions.

The following week, I went to a drum-making workshop in the mountains of Utah by Sundance with Katie Jo. Being in nature, and making my own drum, was really powerful. I had a profound spiritual experience that day.

After two weeks, I was grounded and calm, and ready to start having some conversations with people in Kenya. I was ready for the next step, and I knew where I needed to go for answers.

I sat on the couch in the Jordan River Temple waiting for my name to be called. It was three months since I had returned from Kenya, and I wanted direction and answers about what I was supposed to do in Kenya.

I'm a member of The Church of Jesus Christ of Latter-Day Saints, and the temple is a place where members of my church can go to seek answers to life's challenging questions. This was definitely a challenging question.

I was trying to follow my map (later to realize it was an acronym for me) and there was no X marking the spot where I might begin.

"The scripture trick!" I said in my head, as I spotted a set of scriptures on the table next to me.

I held them in my hands, and focused on what I thought I really needed. At that moment, I needed a beginning, and I needed to know what the big picture was.

For behold, this is my work and my glory—to bring to pass the immortality and eternal life of man.

-Moses 1:39

It was hard to keep from giggling. Really? Moses? Okay. God has a sense of humor.

I hadn't talked to Moses for weeks. In fact, he had made it pretty clear that he had no interest in whatever I was planning to do, and I was told that I had offended him somehow and he hated me.

I put the book down and focused on the message, not really willing to focus on the whole Moses part of the message.

Work, and glory.

Immortality, and eternal life.

That seemed like a nice big picture to work on. I would just go with that.

And then one night a few days later, I was watching a movie with my daughter, and the thought came to my mind, "Email him. Right now. Tell him what you are going to do in Kenya."

I did it. I think it went something like this.

"Dear Moses,

Um, so I know you don't really like me, but I'm going to be probably working with families in Kenya. If I never talk to you again, I think you're an awesome person and I wish you well.

Sincerely, Heidi"

I didn't expect a reply, but one came a few hours later. Moses let me know he thought it was great, and a tentative conversation started about my ideas.

It was five days later that God spoke to me for the first time.

Chapter Five

July 12, 2015
100 Humanitarians

"Go start a group on Facebook called 100 Humanitarians. I'll let you know why," I clearly heard The Voice say.

Um. "Can I get dressed first?"

Maybe you aren't in the habit of talking back to Voices, but I had just gotten out of the shower, was wrapped in a towel, and felt that I needed a little bit more clarification.

"Just do it."

So, I did it. I opened Facebook on my phone and started the group 100 Humanitarians. Just for good measure, I invited a few people to join the group.

"What does 100 Humanitarians mean?" a friend asked.

"I don't know. I'll let you know when I know!" I responded.

A few weeks later a question popped into my head.

What is the power of 100 people?

Ultimately, that question expanded to

> **What is the power of 100 people, working together
> on any project in the world, to
> create positive change?**

And that became the "why" behind everything I'm doing now in Kenya.

Chapter Six

August 2015
A Taste of Kenya

"" **I** went door to door selling pizza coupons for a company that helps with water in Africa, " Ashlyn said. "I tried to give them the money I raised, but they never called me back. Can I give it to you?"

Ashlyn handed over a Ziploc baggy full of what looked like pennies, dimes, nickels, and quarters, and a few dollar bills.

"Wow!" I exclaimed. "Yes, I will use it to start the 100 Humanitarians bank account."

I smiled at Ashlyn's mom, Rebecca, whom I had met in a coaching program at a retreat a few years earlier. "Thank you!"

That was how our funding got started. A teenager going door-to-door trying to help Africa. After I added up the money, it came out to a little over $700. Not a bad start!

My next idea was to host an event that would involve Kenyan food and fundraising in my backyard. I had three weeks to plan it, so I roped in a bunch of friends to help cook and serve, and sold 75 tickets. We had a silent auction, and raised about $1000.

It was a start.

I had planned a scouting trip for November, so that I could go over and decide what projects I wanted to focus on. Opposition was showing up like crazy, and my mindset around whether or not I could really do this was giving me mental whiplash.

As the time to go back to Kenya grew closer, I knew that I was going to need to go in with my heart wide open, ready for miracles.

Chapter Seven

November 5 – 19, 2015
2nd Expedition to Kenya

My flight was delayed, and then delayed again, and then re-routed to Atlanta. I was supposed to meet Melissa* in Amsterdam, and then fly on to Kenya. Instead I ended up spending eight hours at Schipol Airport waiting for a night flight to Nairobi. There are worse airports, and I thought about going out into the city, but it was cold and rainy, and I didn't have a coat with me. I was heading to Kenya, after all.

I inhaled deeply when I walked out of the airplane, so grateful to be back. After getting through the visa line, I went to baggage claim, only to find that one of my bags was missing. A bit of a problem, since we were heading immediately to the Mara for our friend Edith's housewarming party. I filed all of the necessary claims, and went out the doors into the arms of Moses, David, and Christine.

I was home.

We got in the jeep and headed out of town, my lost luggage in the back of my mind as something I would deal with later. This was my first time driving to the Mara, and as the view of the Great Rift Valley emerged, it took my breath away. Why would anyone fly when they could experience this?

Name changed

31

We stopped in Narok to change clothes, and as we drove through the city I said, "Was all this here in March?" We had come from a different direction on that trip, so I had in my head that Narok was three strip malls and a coffee house. I just hadn't turned around the corner to see the rest of a rather huge town. There's a metaphor in there somewhere, but I haven't decided what is just yet.

We picked up Moses's wife and daughter to accompany us to Edith's and I got to snuggle with Shantel on the drive there. We were like peas and carrots. I'm still her favorite Auntie Heidi.

As we drove up to Edith's, I was a bit intimidated by the hundreds of Maasai milling about. This was only my second time to Kenya, very different from my first trip. Mama Helen greeted us at the jeep, and we headed inside. It was fun seeing so many of the people I had met eight months before, and a great start to the trip. I had no idea when my luggage would arrive, and I didn't even know where I was going to sleep that night, but I was beyond happy.

The time came when we needed to pile in the jeep and figure out where we were staying, so I said my temporary farewells and we headed out.

Suddenly, Moses pulled over as he saw an elderly man walking, and said, "I want you to meet my dad."

"Your dad?" I asked.

My mind wandered back to the story I heard in March about his dad, under the pavilion late one night after dinner. He shared that his mom had brought Christianity to that area of the Mara. It was a big stigma and caused the family a lot of problems, especially his dad. It's not really my story to tell, but I was a bit hesitant about meeting him.

I shouldn't have been. As I reached out my hand to say hello, Moses's dad grasped it and held on. His eyes bore into mine for an amount of time that was just slightly awkward before Moses broke our handshake by walking through it. Something happened in that moment, much like my experience in the church in Western Kenya on my first trip.

I took a picture of Moses and his dad, the first one of the two of them ever. We didn't realize at the time that his dad wouldn't have much time left on this earth, and I'm grateful I insisted on taking it. I've had a lot of moments like that, as you can imagine. All captured in pictures.

Moses and his Father

I made a promise to his dad that I helped fulfill on the very spot where this picture was taken, but I didn't realize it until putting it in this book. That's what this experience in Kenya has been. A Master has been at work, weaving a tapestry between all of these experiences, and showing His hand in all of it.

Now, remember that one time I had the worst night of sleep in a mud hut up in the hills? I lied. That place was amazing compared to the guest house we found to stay in that night. Melissa fell asleep as I played beetle ball, killing what seemed like hundreds of bugs flying in the air. It was pouring rain. The mosquito nets had holes. The pillows were flat. Water was dripping from the sink, creating Lake Mara on the floor of the room. It was straight out of a movie.

I managed to get under the mosquito net and under a very thin blanket, and meditated my way to a happy place. In the morning, Melissa said, "Wow, a lot of bugs died during the night."

"I saved your life!" I yelled.

A couple of days later, we were back at Edith's for another party, this time with all women. I sat on a Maasai blanket and listened to everyone around me talk to each other in Maa, the tribal language. At one point I looked up and realized that I was sitting under a tree.

A Wisdom Tree. In Africa. With African women.

I took a picture and when I had internet service again, sent it to Becky Mackintosh and Suzy Gustafson. They were two dear friends I managed to keep from the mass exodus of people who bailed on me after I started 100 Humanitarians.

"I'm under the Wisdom Tree in Africa with Maasai women," the message said.

That day I also went to the baby-naming ceremony for David and his wife Vivian's new baby boy.

"What are you going to name him?" Moses asked.

"Who, me? Why would I name him?" I replied, a bit alarmed.

"David wants you to choose his Maasai name," he responded.

I thought about it and said, "What is the Maasai word for 'happy and smiling'?"

"Oloshipa."

"That's it," I said smiling, thinking of all of the times over the past few months I had asked David how he was doing, only to be answered with "Happy and smiling!"

At the Maasai Naming Ceremony

It was a huge honor to be a part of the ceremony, and to spend some time at David's home with his family. I had many incredible cultural experiences on that trip. And quite a few miracles.

After a few days of adventure on the Mara that included trying to teach Moses and David how to swim, we headed back to Narok. I spent the rest of my time discussing building a cultural center with Moses. He told me if I was serious, that he would contribute the land for it. I was serious.

The following week, Moses and I walked to a grocery store called Naivas. We spent five hours drawing out what the cultural center would look like. That piece of paper is still hanging on my office wall, like a vision board made up of chicken scratch. The guest house we just finished building looks nothing like that paper. It's way more elegant.

An area of Kenya called The Mau Forest is a mountainous region where part of the Maasai tribe lives. It's a beautiful area, but the road to get there is even worse than the road leading to the Mara. We drove up to visit a school called Tenkes, where the elders and leaders were waiting to meet with us.

After hearing some of their challenges, we visited the classrooms. The children were out of school for the holidays. There were 300 children in the community that would be starting up again in January, and very few desks.

The mud hut kitchen where lunch was made for the children each day was falling down, with giant cracks in the mud. I decided that when I returned, we would help build desks, and build a new kitchen. I made a promise to the elders that I would be back.

This time, I got on a plane to fly home with a plan, and that plan was to start bringing people to Kenya on expeditions. I had no idea what I was doing, but "winging it" is my specialty. A few months earlier, my friend Angela Streeter and I were talking about comfort zones and she had said, "I don't understand that idea that everything you want is outside of your comfort zone. I mean, why not just expand it?"

Indeed, why not just expand it?

Mama Helen and Me

Chapter Eight

December 2015
Do You Want to Go to Kenya?

Prior to going to Kenya, I had been on approximately (wait—I mean exactly) two international trips. One was to Mexico in 8th grade. The other was to London with my dad and sister in 2007.

That's it. Are you disappointed? Most people tend to think of me as hugely adventuresome. Nope.

Mexico. London. Kenya 16 times. That's the grand sum of my travels outside the good old U.S.A.

Let's face it, the 16 trips to Kenya often feel like the movie *Groundhog Day* with different people on the trips. Even in Kenya, I'm not really adventuresome.

That has been amusing in many ways, as people assume that I'm the "expert" on Africa, which is a continent, you know. I am basically the "expert" on three communities in one small area of Kenya.

So, in January 2016 when I posted on Facebook and asked, "Do you want to go to Kenya?" I was pretty shocked when people said yes.

The first deposit came in from Brittany. I had met her at a gathering in my friend Kim's basement. Brittany connected me with several of her friends who wanted to go as well. I planned to bring my daughter and Samantha, who had been our babysitter for a few years and had graduated from high school.

Soon, I had more people reaching out to me asking if they could go.

"How many jeeps can I fill?" I asked Moses.

"Two, " was his response.

"What if I have more people? Because I have more people!" I replied.

"Let's just run back to back trips," he said.

"You mean, like a month in Kenya?" I said, a bit astonished.

"Sure."

So, I talked to my husband, whom you haven't been introduced to yet, but you should just know he is a saint, and he said, "Yeah, that's fine."

In the meantime, I was making some waves, and getting messages from people asking when my next trip was, and asking if they could put down deposits.

Panic set in as I realized that I had agreed to take 26 people to Kenya on two back-to-back trips with my ten-year-old daughter, staying for a month.

Oh, boy.

I needed to have a really positive and faith-filled Mindset, and I needed to expect (and pray fervently for) Miracles to make this happen.

Chapter Nine

April 2016
Where's Bomet?

I was three weeks away from flying to Kenya for my first back-to-back expedition (because yes, dear reader, I was crazy enough to do a second one later that fall) and realized that we had really planned out the first team, but not the second team.

For some reason, that had slipped my mind. The first team consisted of mostly single adults and my ten-year-old daughter. It was quite the motley crew, and ultimately a lot of fun. The second team was completely different. It was made up of six homeschooling moms and seven pre-teen kids. And I had no idea what we were doing.

I reached out to Moses and said, "So, what are we doing on the second trip?"

"Well, I think we should go to Bomet in November, "he replied. That was kind of a strange response in retrospect, because it didn't at all answer my question.

"Where's Bomet?" I asked.

"It's the next county over. The Kalenjin Tribe," he said.

A few days later, a friend who was cleaning my house messaged me and said, "A friend of mine works in Kenya. He's in England. I want to connect the two of you."

She connected us, and when I asked him where he worked in Kenya he said, "I work in Bomet."

Well, that's two, right? And these things come in threes, so I sent a message to Heather, and a message to Jenn, both of whom were joining me on the second trip. Both messages said, "Are we going to The Mau or Bomet?"

They both responded with "Bomet." Then Heather said, "Last year when we were in Kenya, a woman named Anita reached out to me to see if we could someday do a project in her village. She's from Bomet."

Yup. That's three.

Heather connected me to Anita, and I connected her to Moses and David, and within a week we had five families identified for us to visit in Bomet for three days on our second trip. Those five families kicked off my dream of working with families in Kenya. We even had a cow donated from my friend, Erin, to give to Facity, a widow with five small children.

Our plans were in place, and it was time for me to start running expeditions to Kenya.

Wheels up.

Chapter Ten

May 12 – 24, 2016
3rd Expedition to Kenya

Dubai is hot. Even in an air-conditioned airport, the heat waves permeate through the windows. After 15 hours of flying, Brittany, Clara and I were exhausted, and had a long layover before we could fly our final leg to Nairobi.

"I love your lashes," I said to Brittany. It's funny the conversations that happen that have nothing to do with humanitarian work.

Here we were, two women and a pre-teen flying through the Middle East en route to Kenya. Nothing to see here. It was pretty surreal.

The three of us were flying in ahead of the team, and since the group mostly consisted of Brittany's friends, she came early, and we designated her as the Team Leader. Brittany had/has really fabulous fake lashes, and I'm not embarrassed to admit that when I got home from those trips, one of the first things I did was get some. First world stuff, right?

I digress.

We landed in Nairobi, and after getting through customs, walked down the ramp where Moses and David were waiting for us. Clara ran to Moses and jumped into his arms with excitement. After my first trip, he had come back with us to the U.S. and she had gotten to meet him. He immediately became her "Uncle Moses" and she was really excited to see him.

Her enthusiasm was infectious. She loved Kenya from the moment her feet touched the ground.

We stayed the night at a hotel that Moses had scouted for our team. I hardly slept, because there was an animal that I still call an elephant monkey (they sound like an elephant, they live in trees, they look nothing like either) that was hollering all night.

After breakfast, we headed to The Giraffe Centre for the first time, and went nuts over feeding the giraffes. It was a beautiful and overcast day. We decided to stop at The Galleria Mall for lunch. Christine had joined us, so there were three Americans, Christine, and the two warriors. They were wearing their full shukas, which is the typical dress for a Maasai, and we got a lot of stares. I don't think that combination happened all that often in Kenya until our teams came along.

Christine and Me at The Giraffe Centre

That night, we headed back to the airport to get the rest of the team. Everyone arrived safely, which was a good sign, and we settled in for our adventure.

Our first stop was a school just outside of Narok, where we held our first Days for Girls workshop with Christine. The 75 girls who attended were from a rescue center called Tasaru.

Tasaru was located in town, and was a refuge for girls who had run from Female Genital Mutilation (FGM) and early marriage.

The girls were quiet and shy at first, but after the workshop and training wrapped up, they swarmed us with hugs and smiles. We spent a lot of time with them that afternoon, getting to know them. It was an amazing beginning to our trip.

Clara with the girls at Tasaru

Clara really loved these girls, and they loved her. They crowded around her and asked tons of questions, and she came alive with excitement. It was her first impression of Kenya, and one that has stayed with her for all of the years we've gone. When I ask her what she most wants to help with in Kenya, she always says the girls.

A couple of days later, we got out of the jeep at the Tenkes School on the Mau, where 300 Maasai children greeted us with singing and dancing.

The 300 children to whom I had promised we would build desks and a kitchen were celebrating our arrival. It seemed as though the entire community had come to join in, as their parents crowded around us as well.

Moses and Me at Tenkes

I was really excited to get my team hammering some nails into wood when I realized that the desks had already been built. Except one.

The kitchen had already been built, and smoke was billowing out of the roof with the promise of lunch in our future.

I was…disappointed. I had envisioned our team working hard, building desks, planting trees with the kids. We had held another A Taste of Kenya event to fundraise for the projects that had sold out with 200 people. I wanted to be able to show them the results of the fundraiser.

At the same time, I saw the expressions on the faces of my team. They were in heaven. They spent the day hugging children and taking selfies.

Eating Goat with the Elders

We had the honor of eating lunch in the bush with the elders, and donated soccer balls and equipment to the school. We also managed to plant 75 trees with the townspeople.

One of the things that EVERY team asks me is, "Will we be able to play with children?"

"Just try to avoid them," I reply.

We left that day with our hearts full. My mind was troubled, though. It felt complete, and I knew that I wouldn't be back to that area on future trips. I was right—I never have gone back.

The elders had asked me if I would build them a soccer field next. I realized that in their minds, 100 Humanitarians had become their new sponsor, but that wasn't the objective I was trying to achieve.

It was a hard lesson—to know of the needs, but not be the one to help. Moses has often had some pretty serious heart-to-heart, come-to-Jesus talks with me about it.

"You can do anything you want, but not all at once," was the advice he gave me. I kept going back to my mindset. Assuming that I could help everyone meant that I would really help no one. We had built desks and the kitchen, and that was what I had promised. Beyond that, I had no vision for that area and what we could do, even though I really loved The Mau and the gentle people who lived there.

Back in those days, we didn't have a lot of funds for projects, so our next stop was Ilturisho, and a picnic at David's house. We spent the afternoon with his family, before heading to Sentrim, the safari camp we had selected. It was tucked away in the woods behind the safari gate, with no wi-fi, so we were going off the grid for a few days.

The rest of the trip included safari, visiting a Maasai village, and singing show tunes. Like I said, it was a really fun group. Our goals had been to provide Days for Girls reusable feminine hygiene kits for 100 women and girls, build 20 desks, a kitchen, and plant 75 trees. We also gave out toothbrushes and tooth-paste, and a lot of soccer balls.

Clara Playing Games at Imani

Our final day, we visited Imani Orphan Care, where we toured the orphanage and donated more soccer balls and equipment. We were learning what we could and couldn't do, in order to stay in alignment with our mission.

I will forever be grateful to the people who put their trust in my vision in Kenya, and joined us on that expedition. I learned a lot from that first experience, when I really didn't know what I was doing. More adventures were coming, because I was only halfway through a back to back trip!

Chapter Eleven

May 26 – June 7, 2016
4th Expedition to Kenya

"Smile!" I said cheerfully. We had stopped off at Mama Helen's house to say hello, before heading back to Nairobi to pick up the second team.

As I was about to take the picture, Mama grabbed Moses's dad, and pulled him in. I had a smirk on my face as I pushed the button. A few months earlier, I had asked Moses if he had any pictures of his parents together.

"That would never happen," was his response.

Just to prove him wrong, I took a selfie with them, too. Then I texted it to him and he said, "How did you do that?"

I'm really quite good at making things happen in Kenya that wouldn't normally happen, and that I normally can't manifest elsewhere.

Mama Helen and Papa Masoi

After we dropped off the first team, we picked up Heather Rangel and her daughter, Sam, to spend a few days with us before the second team arrived.

Heather, Sam, Clara, and I had spent a couple of days relaxing at the safari camp, attending the Sekenani Music Festival at a school, and visiting a family in the northern part of the Mara. We also got trapped in a wicked rainstorm. It seemed like the jeep turned into a boat as we navigated muddy "roads" in the darkness.

I asked David if he had ever experienced driving in water like that. He cheerfully said, "Lots of times!" So, I put my faith in Moses's driving and we made it back to our safari camp.

One night, also during a torrential downpour, we stayed at David's sister's house. We spent the evening mapping out David's genealogy. His father has four wives and David has many siblings, so it was quite the challenge trying to keep it all straight.

The next morning, David shared with me the story of when he was young and responsible for herding cows. A lion attacked the herd, and he had to kill it to defend them. Moments like that made me realize just how different their lives really are.

It was time to go to the airport and pick up the four moms and five kids who were flying to meet us. I was excited for a completely new experience in an area I had never seen. After another trip to the Giraffe Centre (I'll just stop talking about this now, because we go on every expedition!) we headed to Bomet. It was a four- hour drive; the kids were hyper and singing "Waka Waka" the entire way.

The seven kids ranged in age from 10 to 13, both boys and girls. All of them were homeschooled. We divided and conquered, keeping the kids in check with games and a motherlode of snacks. I'm not kidding. I think there are still some of those snacks floating around in Kenya.

Heather organized them all, along with the 37 sizes of Ziploc bags that we had brought along to keep it all straight. Heather is the oldest of 7 kids, and her mad skills came in handy.

After our arrival, we met Anita and her mom, Nancy, and planned out the following day. Our goal was to visit the five families that had been identified who needed our help. We had a lot of supplies for hygiene like toothbrushes and toothpaste, and had donations for cows to start.

Facity and her Five Children

As we walked down the dusty road to Facity's house the next day, we were greeted by many people from her village singing and dancing in greeting. It was beautiful. There were a lot of tears flowing.

Facity's mother-in-law broke down in gratitude. She had been trying to help her with some food, but her ability was dwindling. Her hut was one room, with one bed against the wall. We crowded into the cramped space, and the children with us were silent for the first time as reality set in.

The remainder of our time in Bomet was life-altering. Where the first team had been fun, the second team experienced a rapid succession of miracles.

I have always believed in God, but I met Him in a mud hut in Kenya

Ministering to Julianna

I crawled under the third fence on our walk to Julianna's and said, "Are we there, yet?!" We were on our way to a place that no jeep could get to, so our only option was to walk, and walk, and walk. Well, and engage in Parkour.

When we finally arrived, there was quite the crowd, with Julianna in the middle, completely catatonic. She couldn't speak. She had a hard time making eye contact. The life was ebbing out of her as we stood there.

All of us felt that what we were experiencing was sacred, and that we were all meant to be there for a reason.

We never really learned what was wrong, but for some reason decided it was a bacterial infection. The local doctor hadn't given her family much hope. Anita told us she thought Julianna had hung on because she was told we were coming.

We guided her into her hut and the noise from the children playing outside faded away. As we circled around her to pray, we all felt strongly that we were giving her permission to die. Although there were eight women in the hut, we felt the presence of angels as we prayed and ministered to her. Some experiences are just too sacred for words.

Hours went by, and ultimately we had to go. We left there with the knowledge that she was being left in God's hands. We didn't know what would happen, but we felt she would soon pass.

When I think of the circumstances that had to come together to get us all to that hut in the middle of nowhere in Kenya for that moment, I think about how God works. I thought about how many signs needed to point to Bomet. I thought about how prior to organizing that group, I only knew one of the women in that circle. I learned that day, more than ever, that God is in the details. If he wants me somewhere, I'll get there.

Teaching Vincent to Brush his Teeth

The final family we visited was Mercy and her children. Her oldest son, Vincent, was a sophomore in high school. Mercy was behind on school fees for him, so he was at home. Mercy was shy, and didn't speak much English, but she had a huge smile.

We spent an entertaining few hours there, teaching Vincent how to use a toothbrush, and seeing what was possible for her land. Mercy was working for a farmer, cutting vegetables for around $1/day. Having a cow to provide milk was a much needed source of income, and she was able to receive one a few weeks later.

We agreed that we would sponsor Vincent in school, and also that we would add Julianna's daughters to our education fund.

Our list of students was growing, and my fear of not being able to provide school fees was growing along with them.

Again, my mindset was challenged.

Was I going to trust God and His miracles? Or was I going to say no? On my wall at home was a sign that says,

God never gives you a dream that matches your budget. He's not checking your bank account; he's checking your faith.

As much as I would love to say that every person who has come to Kenya with me becomes a huge supporter of the work there, I can't make that claim. The fact is, many don't stay engaged. Most don't become monthly donors for projects. In fact, from those original expeditions, only two have donated monthly since their trip.

So, I know when I make a promise in Kenya, that come heck or highwater, I am going to have to do what I can to fulfill it. I also know that God is really the one doing the fulfilling. It never fails that I suddenly get an unexpected donation that is exactly what I need, when I need it.

Never.

Once we left Bomet, we were focused on safari and keeping the 7 kids occupied. The boys were able to do warrior training, and one day on the Mara the women in our group had an amazing opportunity to meet with Maasai women and cook dinner with them.

We spent some time talking with them about their challenges. Every woman we hugged had experienced Female Genital Mutilation prior to being married at a very young age. Many of them had residual health problems as a result. Most of them wanted information on how to prevent having children.

But, the joy. They know how to laugh and share stories, even if most of them only speak Maasai. The connections that were created in such a short time were amazing, but women often are able to come together in miraculous ways.

At one point, Heather, Jenn and I snuck away and walked out to the ground where Moses had told me that the Cultural Centre would be built. We said a prayer of dedication, with a hope that someday we would see it built. As we prayed, we felt surrounded by angels and ancestors who were there to support the Maasai. The work had begun.

And our month in Kenya had ended.

"I had come to Africa to fulfill a promise. I was to leave Africa connected to my own soul."

-Denis Waitley, Safari to the Soul

Chapter Twelve

July 2016
A Taste of Kenya #3

"You should come to the United States for our next A Taste of Kenya," I texted Moses one day, a few weeks after I got home from my month- long adventure. On a whim. I do way too many things on a whim. Someone should really stage an intervention.

We started the long and exhausting paperwork and interview process, ending in Moses saying, "My application was approved, and I was able to get a five-year visa! I almost didn't get it, though. I was late to the interview, and didn't have cash, and I basically convinced the person to give me the visa. I had to run to the gate to get cash from David, and they almost didn't let me back in."

If I had a dollar every time Moses reported something similar, I'd be able to retire to a beach in Bora Bora. Although truthfully, I would be pretty bored.

A few days later, David went through the same process and was denied. They told him he didn't have strong enough ties to Kenya, although he was born there, has two wives and six kids, and has never left the country.

(People always ask me when David is going to come. We've tried to get his visa four times and it has been denied every time.)

I scheduled Moses's flight to come in five weeks before our expedition that fall, so that we could do a bunch of different events. He was excited, and less than thrilled to be coming by himself. I was excited to have him dance, sing, and jump for everyone in Utah.

Remember, A Taste of Kenya was an event I had put on a couple of times to fundraise for our projects. The first one was in my backyard. We set up tables, made Kenyan food, and about 75 people came. For a first event, it was pretty fun.

The second go round was at an event center downtown. We sold out four days ahead of the event, and it was kind of boring. I mean, I did my best, but organizing, managing, emceeing, and fundraising should not be left to one person. Everyone knew I was winging it, but it was still a success.

For my third attempt, I booked more musical performers. All of them said, "You should call Alex Boye. He would be perfect for this."

Alex Boye is a performer who does a lot of cover songs and "Africanizes" them. One of his most popular videos on YouTube is "Circle of Life" from *The Lion King* with millions of views. He lives locally, and is well known, so I figured I'd take a chance.

I reached out on Alex's website to talk to him about it, but never got a response, so I gave up and just started selling tickets with the line up of Jennifer Marco, Cactus Jack, and Afro Fusion. I was really excited for it. We had decided to hold it at Club 90 after the owner, Rachelle Halling-Valdez, offered it to us.

There was a lot of work to do, and many miracles ahead that you will read about. Suffice it to say, what happened for this event was a clear message from God that we were on the right path, even though we were being challenged constantly with opposition.

There is a price to become truly acquainted with God, and I was willing to pay it.

Chapter Thirteen

August 2016
Thy People Shall Be My People
(Ruth 1: 16-20)

"**Y**ou need to decide where your focus will be. You can't work everywhere in Kenya, " the text from Moses said.

I was pretty frustrated, but Moses was right. My focus had been pretty scattered. I was trying to take on way more than I could handle, and it was causing contention between us.

I had really loved Bomet and loved the people there, but from the beginning I knew that the cultural center was a priority, and that was on the Mara. So far I had had no success fundraising for it. No one wanted to build a building. Everyone wanted to donate cows, goats, and hygiene kits.

The Church of Jesus Christ of Latter-Day Saints has weekly worship at chapels, but we have temples where covenants are made for ourselves and on behalf of our ancestors. Years earlier before I got married, I had had the opportunity to be a temple worker in the Washington, DC Temple. I had often gone and implemented "The Scripture Trick" in which I would grab the scriptures and open them after asking a question. Since it had worked for me in the beginning when I got the answer that I needed to work with Moses, I figured it would work again.

"I'm going to the temple, "I texted back. "When I come out, I'll know my answer."

As I sat in the temple pondering that day, I looked around for a Book of Mormon. There were none to be found. Strange. Everywhere I looked there were Bibles. My faith uses the Bible extensively, but it was just a surprise, because I usually open the Book of Mormon for my scripture trick.

I picked up the Bible and said a short prayer. It opened to Ruth, Chapter One.

> **16** *And Ruth said, Entreat me not to leave thee, or to return from* [a]***following*** *after thee: for whither thou goest, I will* [b]***go***; *and where thou lodgest, I will lodge: thy* [c]***people*** *shall be my people, and thy God my* [d]***God***:
>
> **17** *Where thou diest, will I die, and there will I be buried: the Lord do so to me, and more also, if ought but death part thee and me.*

Okay, I thought. But that doesn't really answer my question. Which tribe is my focus? Now, caveat: I wasn't looking for which tribe to be the focus for 100 Humanitarians. This was a personal focus, not a collective one.

"Keep reading," the Voice said.

So, I kept reading, and when I stopped, I finished up my work at the temple and went outside.

"I have my answer," I sent the text to Moses. "My focus is the Maasai. Specifically the Mara."

18 *When she saw that she was* ᵃ**steadfastly** *minded to go with her, then she left speaking unto her.*

19 ˢ*So they two went until they came to Beth-lehem. And it came to pass, when they were come to Beth-lehem, that all the city was moved about them, and they said, Is this Naomi?*

20 *And she said unto them, Call me not* ᵃ**Naomi***, call me* ᵇ**Mara***: for the Almighty hath dealt very bitterly with me.*

Once again, God couldn't have been more clear with me.

"What are we calling the Cultural Center?" I asked Moses.

"It's the Emparnat Cultural Centre," he said. "You're the person. Emparnat is the place."

A place of wisdom, where people gather.

Perfect.

Chapter Fourteen

September 2016
Moses Arrives in the U.S.

"When does Moses arrive?" Heather messaged me. "I have free tickets to an Alex Boye concert. It would be cool if he met Moses."

Mic drop.

The concert was just a few hours after Moses was scheduled to land in Salt Lake City, but I wasn't going to miss this chance, so I grabbed the tickets, told Moses to get his shuka on, fed him with a hamburger, French fries, and a coke, and we headed downtown.

Moses dozed through the first part of the concert, but when Alex came on, we all moved forward. I just knew that Alex would see Moses and the sea would part and…well, I wasn't sure what would happen, but I had a feeling it would be cool.

None of that happened. I mean, it happened, but not right away, because the theater was dark, so Alex couldn't look out and see that a Maasai was sitting in the audience. You can tell that I think Maasai warriors are pretty cool. I will tell you that Moses doesn't love that I love to parade around a Maasai warrior. It's been a battle at times over the years.

I digress. Again. I'm a digresser.

After the concert, we walked out, and I just had this feeling that if we went back into the auditorium, magic would occur. We walked back in, where Alex and his crew were cleaning up.

"Maasai!" Alex shouted from the stage.

The sea parted (just kidding, but we were walking down the aisle so it kind of felt like that) and we all made introductions. As we talked, Alex said, "How long are you here? You should come tomorrow and be in a video with me."

Oh, well, okay. I mean, why not?

The next day we drove to Kaz's drum shop and filmed a video for one of Alex's clients. To my knowledge that video was never released, but it inspired us to talk about doing another video for one of Alex's songs at a later date.

Time went on, and we went to various events where Moses would remind me that he is neither a singer nor a dancer, and why did I keep scheduling him for stuff that required singing and dancing? I later apologized after I got back to Kenya and saw the Wall of Warriors and remembered that their music is more of a call and response than a solo gig.

Oh, I need to share another part of this story.

Duh.

There's a Maasai gospel singer named Stephen Leken that I love in Kenya, and I hunted him down on Facebook, messaged him, and asked him if he would be willing to perform at a concert during our October expedition. I'm not really sure what I was thinking, but it seemed like it would be fun.

Moses asked if I was really serious about doing a concert, and casually said, "I wonder if we could get Lemarti there."

Lemarti? LEMARTI!

Every ringtone in Kenya is a Lemarti song. Okay, not true. Every ringtone on the Maasai Mara is a Lemarti song. He's like the Bob Marley of Kenya, and in fact he often wears Bob Marley inspired clothes, so that is a true statement in more than one way.

Moses started messaging him, and after a conversation back and forth, broke into a grin across the table from me at a Mexican restaurant and said, "He said he would do it." Moses doesn't really get excited. But he was excited that day, and couldn't hold back his smiles.

A few minutes later, his expression changed to shock.

"Look at this, "he said.

He held out his phone and on the screen I saw The Circle of Life video on YouTube with Alex Boye and…Lemarti.

It turned out that a couple of years earlier, Alex had gone to Kenya to film the video, and invited Lemarti to be in it. I mean, what are the odds? All I could think of was what mountains God had to move for this to all come together.

A week later, Alex texted me and asked if we could do the video that coming Saturday, which happened to be the day of A Taste of Kenya. I told him the situation, and he said, "Okay, so what if we film during the day, and we wind up the video at A Taste of Kenya and I'll perform."

Oh, okay. That's a great idea.

And that is exactly what happened. We spent the day filming, I went live on Facebook telling everyone that we were at Alex Boye's house dressing him up as a Maasai, and A Taste of Kenya sold out quickly.

Alex, Moses and Me Filming Promised Land

There's a whole thing with the video about a potbelly pig and wandering through downtown Salt Lake City looking for Al Fox Carraway, but just go watch the video on YouTube.

It's called Promised Land. Originally Alex promised he would promote 100 Humanitarians at the end of the video, but he didn't. That was a big bummer. It was still fun, though.

Alex Boye Performed at A Taste of Kenya

Chapter Fifteen

Oct 27 – Nov 8, 2016
5th Expedition to Kenya

"Her name is Heidi Jena Masoi, " the message said. I had been kidding when I subtly suggested that Moses name his new daughter after me when she was born a few months earlier.

The first time I held her, she was bundled up in 64 layers of clothing and snowsuits, which is often how babies in Kenya are wrapped up. I was at the airport waiting for Moses's family waiting for his flight to arrive. He had been in the U.S. but we had been in separate flights, and his came in after mine.

As I loved on my namesake, I could feel her heartbeat. Strange since it was through all of those layers. The heart knows. She felt like one of my own children, and I knew that she would be a part of my life.

The Two Heidis

Shantel danced and sang and chattered as we waited, and then broke out into a run when her daddy arrived. Mama Helen was there with a big gourd of yogurt, or curdled milk that had been curdling since Moses had left. Probiotics at its best. I was voluntold to try it. I think that moment is why I hardly get sick now. My immune system agreed to stay healthy if I agreed not to eat that yogurt again.

Moses and the Yogurt

The team arrived in Kenya and we headed immediately to the Mara in order to get everything ready for the concert with

Lemarti. He had told us that he was bringing his fiancé, Resh, and two other singers, Saning'o and Jeff Ole Kishau, with him. David had added Pastor Ben, a gospel singer from one of the areas we would start working in on the second trip later that fall (I ran two back to back trips in 2016. I won't do that, again.)

Meeting Lemarti

Add in Stephen Leken, and we had a pretty incredible line-up. We rented a couple of big tents and a sound system, and invited a few local dignitaries. It was the first time that Lemarti had performed on the Mara, so about 500 people showed up for the concert.

Prior to the concert starting, we delivered a cow to a family near Nkoilale who had a daughter that had run from early marriage. Ndee had a baby, and her father had agreed to let her stay, but wouldn't support her. She wanted to go back to school, so we agreed we would sponsor her, if her mother could take care of the baby.

After meeting the family, we headed over to the cultural center grounds for the concert. The team made a ton of food with some of the local women, and the concert went long into the afternoon and evening.

It was really fun, and I saw a lot of friends. But it was the wrong expedition team for that concert. As awesome as it was for me, it was pretty boring for them, and a few expressed that they wondered why they were there. The challenge was the timing of the concert. I learned that it really is better to go to the Mara at the end of an expedition and not the beginning.

Lemarti Performs on the Mara for the First Time

The weather was really hot and dry that year. The worst I had seen it. Kenya was experiencing a terrible drought, and it was dusty. Most of the trees and bushes were drooping and dead. Our plan for that trip was to plant trees. It was awful.

To make it even worse, one of the women had another agenda in mind and had been talking about what she wanted to do. It wasn't the objective for the trip, but trying to explain that to the group was difficult. The whole expedition felt misaligned and off.

Ultimately, it was a blessing, because she set up a Days for Girls enterprise in Bomet, but it caused a lot of division and confusion with the team, because they wanted to go, too. I suggested at the end of the trip that she start her own organization, and we parted ways. It was a big awakening to me that I hadn't cast the right vision for the trip. A lesson I would learn over and over again.

Lemarti said that he and his friends wanted to stay with our team after the concert, go on safari, and hang out for a few days. David had built a house in his village, Ilturisho, so we were scheduled to attend his housewarming party. That ended up being really cool for David to have all of those performers at his party. Our YouTube channel loved the videos. If I'm famous at all, anywhere in the world, it's because I helped bring Lemarti to the Mara.

Lemarti Performing on Safari

That was the first trip that Becky Mackintosh came with me, and we got to take a picture under The Wisdom Tree in Africa. I had met Becky while working for "Penny," who had actually promised to take both of us to Africa. It was a fun moment for us, and a preview of what was to come for Becky in Kenya.

After the Mara, we headed to Narok, where we visited the girls from Tasaru, the rescue center where we did our first workshop, and hosted another reusable feminine hygiene workshop for the girls who hadn't received kits from us a few months earlier. We also visited Imani again, and an orphanage for teen boys. The kids were out of school; we heard some heartbreaking stories.

I connected with a boy named Sam on that trip, and it reaffirmed in my mind that the work I hoped to do would impact the next generation.

When all was said and done, we didn't do much service on that trip. I look back and realize that what was accomplished was building a foundational relationship with the community by hosting the concert.

Perhaps equally as important for the work we needed to do long term.

After dropping off the team, I spent a couple of days in Nairobi with Jen, who was my team lead for the second of my back-to-back trips that fall. I think we mostly slept. I was pretty exhausted from the heat, and taking a team of 15 women was a bit of drama. I mean, organizing expeditions is not my strong suit, to be honest. I didn't set out to do it in life.

One of my biggest challenges with travel is a condition that I have called lymphedema in my lower legs. I've had it since I was a young teenager, and it has gotten worse over the years with having children. Managing my health on expeditions is critical, and that often means that I have to scale back. At this point in my journey, I didn't have a lot of help, and I didn't know how to ask for it. That was a big mistake early on. Had I known better what I was doing, I could have avoided many issues.

However, I'm really there for the projects and the people, and I have learned to forgive myself for not knowing what I didn't know. I've learned over the years not to let it get to me as much, when I have inevitably disappointed someone. Some people come and they absolutely love Kenya, and it becomes their thing, too. Others don't. I'm grateful for all of them. They are all part of the journey.

Chapter Sixteen

November 10 – 22, 2016
6th Expedition to Kenya

After we picked up the next team in Nairobi, we headed to a nightclub on the outskirts of the city. Yep, you read that right. We had been invited to Jeff Ole Kishau's CD launch for Maasai night. It was a very weird way to start an expedition. The party started at 6pm and went until 6am, and after cutting a cake at around 3am, we were ready to go back to the hotel.

I actually texted my husband and said, "I just danced on stage with a half-naked warrior named Saningo."

He wrote back, "Sounds like a normal day for you."

I can't tell you how often I say the words, "I'm not sure why a middle-aged mom from Utah was chosen to do all of this."

But there it was, another day, another cake to cut, another strange experience that would never happen to me in the U.S. After sleeping in a bit, we headed to our hotel in Suswa. The first family that we were going to visit was nearby. It was a great hotel with one glaring exception. There was a nightclub right next to it. As in, right in the parking lot. Said nightclub liked to play music all.night.long.

We had started the Business Box for Families in Bomet in May, and expanded to a few families on the Mara. Our next community that we were going to was Ntulele/Suswa, where more families had been identified for us to work with. This was Pastor Ben's congregation, so he had planned which families we would be working with.

We didn't get a lot of sleep those first few days.

My friend Holly came on that trip with her daughter, Sabrina. Holly and I had grown up together in Phoenix, and Sabrina had sewn 100 Days for Girls kits and brought them for her Girl Scout Gold Project. We were able to do a workshop for the women at Pastor Ben's church, and provided Days for Girls kits to the families we visited. It was cool to experience that.

One day, as we headed to Paster Ben's house, we came up on a blockade in the road. There were tires burning—a protest was happening. Moses was able to get through, but by the time we got there, we were surrounded. There were eight of us plus David in the jeep. It was hot, and cars and jeeps were backed up for kilometers behind us.

We sat there for about an hour, right at the front of the action, at which point Gigi threatened that she would use a bottle for a restroom in the jeep if we didn't find an alternative option. When we suggested that idea to David, he wasn't on board. He arranged with the Rangers who were there to manage the protest to have us go up a little hill and create our own make-shift latrine, and off we went. We were told to be quick because they were going to use tear gas.

Eight American women walking up a hill make quite the spectacle. The Rangers looked a bit nervous, having not real-ized that we were in the jeep that was front and center. As I walked back, I gestured to the women behind me and said to the Ranger, "Really? Tear gas?"

He briefly looked at me, and I looked directly at him. We got back in the jeep, and suddenly the whole protest ended, and we drove right through. Another lesson I learned that day. Kenyans respect tourists, and they don't want a scandal in their country.

Every time we drive past the area on the road that it happened, I give a small prayer of gratitude that it didn't escalate into a more dangerous situation. While I never felt unsafe for a moment, I definitely felt angels protecting us.

As we continued down the road to deliver a cow to a family, we said a prayer of gratitude. It's not a story I share often, because I never want people to fear coming to Kenya. However, the reality is that it is a developing country, and that brings challenges and corruption.

There was palpable relief when we arrived at Pastor Ben's and could continue our work. Elizabeth, whose husband was in prison, was a mother of three daughters. She had a lot of land and space for a garden, but lacked the resources to use it effectively. We donated a cow to her, that we walked down the road, again to a community of people singing.

Donating a Cow to Elizabeth

A word about gratitude and Kenyans. All of their gratitude is for God and Jesus Christ. As I said before, I always believed in God, but met him in a mud hut. He has continued to reveal Himself to me on every expedition, and on many occasions in between. My ability to hear and feel inspiration and guidance has expanded, and continues to expand.

Somewhere along this journey, I read the book *Kisses from Katie*, about a woman who literally gave up her whole life to work in Uganda. Her faith inspired me, and kept me going. I don't want to say that I test God, but I probably do. Often.

Intertwined with our adventures was the making of a documentary about what we had done so far in Kenya. Shaison was an Indian filmmaker who had joined us to help tell the story of 100 Humanitarians. At that point, I had taken 50 people to Kenya, so we were halfway to the power of 100. He got some great footage, but the story wasn't there, yet. We had helped some families, but we didn't know the outcome of our efforts. We were really just going on faith that it would work, having at that point donated quite a few very expensive cows.

The Oiboo Family

Our final stop was at the Oiboo family. There were two wives and 16 children, and before we went to their homes, we stopped by the market to buy a goat. We named the goat Mother Becci, and I kissed her for good luck.

All of these families had a huge impact on me, and even though we have gone on to work with hundreds, I know and remember all of their names. I see their faces, and pray for them. They will always hold my heart, because they helped us figure all of this out.

The end of that trip was rough and painful. I'll be honest, I went home very discouraged, and ready to quit. I was also extremely exhausted, having spent two months in 2016 navigating 50 people through Kenya. My emotions were all over the place, and it had taken its toll. And then God reminded me to watch for the miracles.

Chapter Seventeen

December 2016
Arbinger Institute Training

"Can you clear your schedule next week for four days? It's important!" Shaun's text came in late in a Friday afternoon, and I laughed at the thought. Clear my schedule? Four days in December? Can ANYONE do that?

Within 48 hours my schedule was clear, and I was on my way to the Tanner Building at BYU to take the Arbinger Institute Training for Non-profits, hosted by the Forever Young Foundation.

A few weeks before, I had gotten home from leading my fourth expedition to Kenya that year, and I was done. Finished. Ready to never set foot in the country again if I could avoid it. On the way home I had found out that several of our team members had gotten drunk with the staff at the safari camp. I had thrown my heart and soul into taking 50 people to Kenya over the year, and was fed up with it all.

At that point, it had been over a year since my experience in the booth at Paradise Bakery with my once best friend. I wondered if I had made a huge mistake. Perhaps I should have simply stayed with the "inner circle" instead of trying to follow my heart.

It was starting to feel that for every miracle, there was a huge pile of opposition in between. I wasn't sure what the next few days would entail, but if I was going to continue, it would need to be life-altering. It was my last shot. If I didn't get some sort of direction, my plan was to tear up that MAP of mine and let families in Kenya fend for themselves, because I obviously wasn't the right person to lead.

To put things in perspective, the last straw was being accused of stealing a cow by a donor. Well, not actually the cow, but the money for the cow.

Seriously. At that point I had invested thousands of hours and dollars in building a non-profit that wasn't paying me a salary. I had been rejected by friends. My family thought I was nuts. I had been away from my husband and son for two months out of that year. Enough, already.

Over the next four days in the training, I realized everything that I had been doing wrong. From being willing to go with the flow and do whatever anyone wanted to do in Kenya, to not clearly defining the purpose and vision of the organization. I hadn't been a leader. Just the opposite. And the organization needed a leader.

Was I ready to be that leader? I had spent much of my life following the crowd and putting people on pedestals. This was going to be a bit of a stretch for me, but if God wanted me to do it, I guess I would go back.

But first, I needed to write a few apology letters.

*The names have been changed.

Letter #1
Dear Penny

In October 2012 I went to an event where my business coach Kim was speaking. That's where I met Penny. Oddly enough, that's where I first saw Jason Hewlett perform, who later helped me write my first book. Are you seeing how all of these different mentors (both good and bad) showed up because of each other? That's why today I just honor them all. I wouldn't have had the good without the bad.

Penny ran an organization I thought was destined to change the world. Mostly because she told me that it would. Once I peeled back the onion layers, I realized that most of what she told me was fraudulent. The scary thing was how much she believed her own lies.

She invited me to work for her organization and I was all in. Literally. For the next seven months I worked about 60 hours a week buying into whatever she said. And then I started to wake up to her lies and manipulations.

So I quit, and I sued her for not paying me. I won.

One of the things she had promised me was a trip to Africa. She shared a story about women under The Wisdom Tree in Africa that inspired me. When the case settled and I got my check, I used that money to sign up for my first trip to Kenya. I guess in the end, she did take me to Africa.

It wasn't all bad. I made a lot of incredible friends from that experience, including Becky Mackintosh, Suzy Gustafson, Bridget Cook-Burch, and several other women who have been a big part of my journey. But, I was ready for closure.

During the 2016 Arbinger Institute Training, I realized that I wanted her to know how I used the money. Oddly, I wanted her to think better of me, because I hate loss of approval from people. So I wrote the letter. I apologized for any role I played in creating drama, and I wished her well.

She wrote back, telling me just how much I had wronged her and magnanimously forgave me. It made me laugh, but I got over it. That was the purpose of the letter—closure.

Letter #2
Dear Melissa

After my great rejection from the "Inner Circle" I realized that I needed to go back to Kenya to do a bit of scouting, and figure out what was possible for me there. My friend Melissa was moving over, so I went to help her get settled in.

I was excited about the option to work with her because she would be boots on the ground. We had a great trip and I left feeling all mushy inside about it. I'm a connector, and I don't love doing things by myself. I saw her as a leader.

When I got home, I started throwing it out to the world that I was going to take people to Kenya. A few people signed up for a trip the following May. Then a few more signed up, and it snowballed. We had to split the trips and plan back-to-back expeditions with 13 people on each trip.

When I talked with Melissa about it, she said she wouldn't be able to help me on my trip, because she would be out of the country. That threw me for a loop, but plane tickets and hotels were already booked, so I decided I would just move forward. We could collaborate on future trips.

It got pretty awkward and weird between us. I hosted a fundraising event. Because she was in the U.S. for it, I invited her up onto the stage to speak. When I went to hug her, she sidestepped me. I was humiliated.

Melissa messaged me and told me that I had "stolen" her clients, who thought they were signing up for a trip with her, but instead signed up for mine. I was horrified, and paid her a commission for it, only to find out later that she had lied. The people she claimed had "accidentally" signed up with me had never intended to sign up with her.

I was furious about it, and ultimately just stopped responding to messages from her. Not the best way to handle it, but I'm a different person now.

As part of my Arbinger training, I wrote her a letter, apologizing for my part in the misunderstanding. She never responded. I found out other ways that she was trying to sabotage what I was doing, so I left it at that. However, I at least felt better that I tried to resolve it at one point.

Letter #3

Dear Lou

The letter to Lou was different. Our friendship had nothing to do with Kenya, and actually started years before I ever jumped into the entrepreneur world. She lived across the street, and for many years we were the best of friends.

She went through some hard times and I got caught up in the drama and bowed out. That had been a few years earlier, and since I was writing letters, I figured I would write one to her as well. The result was much different.

I was really nervous when I hit Send. Writing these letters was not easy, and I geared up for rejection on all of them.

Twenty-four hours after I sent the email to her, there was a knock at the door. My mother answered and called upstairs, "Heidi, Lou's here!" My heart started pounding and I hoped that she wasn't there to yell at me.

On the contrary. I came down the stairs and she threw her arms around me and said, "Of course I forgive you." We talked for three hours after that, and just caught up. It was really peaceful, and healing. Isn't that the best? I wish I had sent the email years earlier, but maybe we both needed to be ready for it. God's timing is always best. That's something Kenyans tell me often.

Letter #4
Dear Amy

I saved the final letter for Amy, the woman who had kicked me out of her "Inner Circle" while I ate a cookie at Paradise Bakery (I haven't gone back since.)

Again, I apologized not for my behavior, but for the role I played in creating the contention and drama after we got back from my first trip to Kenya. While I still didn't understand what had changed, I had accepted it. In this case, it might have still been a little too raw, but I was all in for Arbinger's method and still felt it was important to move forward.

Her reply wasn't super encouraging, but it started a back and forth conversation that I thought at least brought us to a place of neutral. I didn't expect a friendship, but I at least felt that if I ran into her somewhere that I wouldn't be turning around and running away.

The neutrality stuck until March of 2018 when we had a conversation that I thought was lighthearted and she took it a completely different way and the rage set in, again. At that point, it just became abusive and toxic. I blocked her everywhere and considered it complete. When I think about her, I send her love.

I learned a great deal from the experience of writing these letters. It set me free from some of the heavy things that had been weighing on me. A big part of it was forgiveness, and just letting the past be the past. I was so grateful that I cleared my schedule for the training, and now I recommend that every leader of non-profits go through it.

Chapter Eighteen

March 12 – 22, 2017
7th Expedition to Kenya

I was reluctant to go back to Kenya after the turmoil of fall 2016, but my husband's cousin, Michelle, convinced me, along with my experience at the Arbinger Institute Training. Back in 2015 on my first trip, I asked our director if he had ever heard of square foot gardens. Not only had he heard of them, he had learned how to build them in Utah with the same instructor I had!

Our team was small. We had just four women and one jeep, and I was happy with that. Moses and David had been invited to go to England for a marketing training for safari drivers, and had plans to leave just a few days after we arrived, so John was going to mostly be driving us.

We started our journey by visiting Christine's sewing enterprise in a suburb of Nairobi where it wasn't common to see Americans in safari jeeps.

Normally, we don't take teams into areas like this because of safety, but we were a small group and we had three Maasai warriors with us, so we felt okay about it. (I'm writing this so that my mom doesn't worry. She still thinks I am going to be eaten by a lion, and she's been to Kenya twice!)

The Workshop at Bondeni School

We visited a school called Bondeni, where we hosted a feminine hygiene workshop with the 7th and 8th grade girls.

Our first stop was to go back to Suswa and start our new projects. My hope was that this trip would be peaceful and help me get motivated to keep going.

We decided that we would build garden boxes for seven different families. The previous November, we had opened a new area in Ntulele with a few families in Pastor Ben's congregation.

Pastor Ben's church was up the mountain into the Mau Forest, and our team had the chance to help prepare the ground to rebuild a new and bigger building. By building, I mean corrugated tin walls, but it was still bigger.

The Mau is a lovely, peaceful part of Kenya. In that area, there are the Mau Maasai, and the Mara Maasai. Both from the same tribe, but a bit different in how they live. The Mau Maasai grow crops, where the Mara Maasai are more pastoral.

We arrived at our hotel in Suswa, and the next day went to the lumber and hardware store to get the wood for the boxes. Our first stop was at the home of another family we had visited the previous year. Part of our stipulation for building the boxes, was that the family would come and take part to learn how to use them. Sadly, this family didn't show up. Ultimately, we ended up dropping them. Stewardship and collaboration are essential requirements for us.

Building Our First Garden Box

The second garden box was at the Oiboo's house. John was a great help in explaining the concept to the family. His mom had grown gardens before, so he had experience with them. As a thank you, the Oiboos gave us a chicken. I thought it was a "We are going to give you a chicken, but we'll keep it here for you" situation. It wasn't. Moses put the chicken in the jeep and let us know that would be dinner.

Receiving Kuku Moses

We actually didn't believe him, so we named the chicken Kuku Moses ("Chicken Moses" in Swahili). He spent the rest of the day at Michelle's feet in the jeep, occasionally squawking and freaking us out.

Our final destination was Elizabeth's. She had an area mapped out for a garden, so we had the perfect place to put it, without having to worry about fencing to keep animals out.

Our goal was to try to teach them an efficient way to garden, using crop rotation and less water.

The following year, we learned that the garden boxes were being eaten by termites. Fortunately, we were presented with another solution, but that comes later in the story.

"Tomorrow, we are going to go to Narok, " Moses announced.

I pulled him aside. "When are you leaving for the airport?" I asked.

He lowered his eyes and said, "I'm not going. If David's visa comes through, I'll send him."

"Why aren't you going?!" I asked.

Over the previous couple of days, I had noticed that both Moses and David were reluctant to leave. David had said to me, "How can I leave, when you are in Kenya?"

It turned out that David's visa was denied. The next day, they were both a lot happier, but it wasn't long before we had some awful news that made us grateful they had stayed.

I'll never forget reading the text from Moses, because he was sitting right behind me in the jeep.

"My dad's diagnosis came. He has liver cancer."

My heart sunk. I knew what that meant for an old shepherd in his 80s. Though I really hadn't known the Masoi family very long, I had begun to understand the role of elders in the community.

The previous November, his dad had come over to me and simply took my hand in his. That had become our routine every time I saw him that trip. He would just come and hold my hand. I thought it was strange, but that was just our relationship. We didn't speak the same language, but somehow we communicated anyway.

After a stop in Narok so that I could snuggle with Shantel and Baby Heidi, who was FINALLY warming up to me, we headed to the Mara for rest and safari. My friend, Becky Rogers, joined us from Ghana, where she had moved her family a few months earlier to run Families Mentoring Families. We have an East-West Africa thing going on.

Becky Rogers Joins the Team

We continued our projects over the next few days. One afternoon we stopped at Mama Helen's after safari. Moses had asked me to look at his father's medical paperwork and let him know what I thought about it. As I read the diagnosis, I knew that I would be saying goodbye to him that day.

I asked if I could see him, and he came into the small living room. He was emaciated and weak, but sat down next to me and took my hand. For the next half hour, I listened to the family talk, and just tuned into his spirit, so that I could recognize when he was around me in the future.

Quietly, in my head I asked him, "What do you need me to do?"

I felt his response clearly. He looked at Mama Helen and said, "I need you to help take care of her."

I squeezed his hand in acknowledgement. Soon it was time to go, and holding back the tears, I hugged him and said, "Kaanyor Oleng."

I often think about my Maasai father. It's hard not to. He's been very active in my life since he passed away, and I often see how he is helping us in Kenya. It's just in little ways that no one else would notice, but I know he is present.

Sometimes, I'll even say, "I see what you did there." Then I feel him pat my hand.

"Nemparnat, " He says. "That's the right name for you."

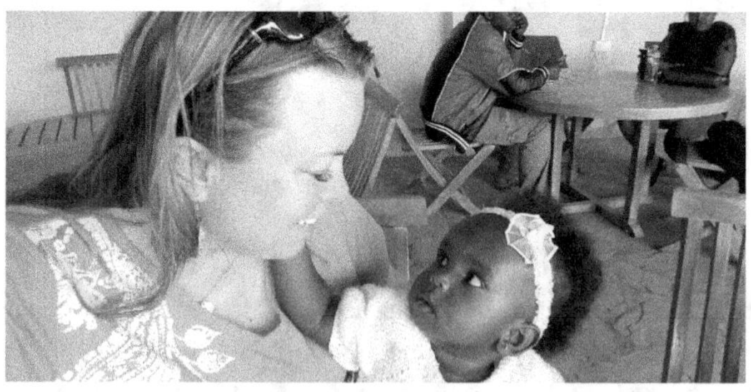

Baby Heidi and Me

We wrapped up the trip having built 7 garden boxes with 7 families. Our garden project had begun, and my heart had been healed. That may sound dramatic, but this type of work really does bring tremendous personal opposition, and I deal with a lot of head trash – telling me I'm not good enough to do this.

I'm grateful that over the years I've been gathering emotional tools and resilience from coaches and mentors to help me get through it all. If you are thinking about starting a non-profit, especially in another country, gear up.

You should also know that people show up just when you need it. Sometimes that is a friend with supportive words, and sometimes that is an unexpected donation that is the exact amount needed. If I have learned a prevailing truth in all of this, it is that God provides. He just likes to let other people be His hands.

Chapter Nineteen

May 2017
A Taste of Kenya #4
All is Well

Sometimes I get messages from random people that I've been Facebook friends with for a while. In 2016, I got a message from Wendy Bunnell, asking if I was interested in writing a story for a book that she was putting together called *Success Through Failing*. As we talked, I suggested that she also talk with Christine and Anita about writing a chapter about their experiences in Kenya.

I also convinced her to plan for Kenya in June 2017 and to bring her son.

The book launched and hit #1 on Amazon the same weekend that we held The Success Summit to go along with the book. A series of miracles occurred that enabled us to get Anita a visa to come to the U.S. for the event. It was incredible to be able to stand side by side with her and speak to women about what we had been able to do in Kenya.

Since Wendy was coming with us to Kenya, and Wendy rarely does anything small, she decided to host A Taste of Kenya in Vernal, Utah. Vernal is a small town about three hours away from Salt Lake City. I had only been once the year before, when

Kaci had thrown the event "Koncert for Kenya" to raise money for Elizabeth's cow.

I drove to Vernal and met up with Vilia, the board chair and accountant for 100 Humanitarians. She's also a chef and a chocolateur. Seriously, you would just go nuts over her food. Okay, back to the story.

The event was hugely successful. Wendy's efforts had led to a sold out crowd, and the auction raised several thousand dollars. It was a really fun weekend hanging out with friends, cooking food, and planning for the trip.

On Sunday, I started the three-hour drive home. I knew I wouldn't get back in time for church, and I wanted to do something that day that would be memorable, so I decided to stop in Altamont at the cemetery where my oldest cousin Mark is buried. I hadn't been there since college, so I wasn't totally sure I would be able to find the grave, but it was worth a try.

It was cold and overcast. After a few minutes of searching, I found Mark's headstone and sat down in front of it. I looked at his name, and I thought about my experience when he passed away in 1990 and how it had impacted my family. Moses's dad was on my mind. He had been in the hospital, and I knew that it was only a matter of time before he would pass on.

Mark has a Scottish piper on his headstone, and I looked at the plaid kilt and thought of the Maasai shuka, a Scottish plaid fabric that is in their clothing and blankets. "Mark, are you helping me in Kenya?" I asked out loud.

I looked up as the wind suddenly started rushing through the trees, and I kid you not, I responded with, "Oh, come on! You can do better than that!"

Mark was just 24 years old when he died. I was a few weeks away from starting at BYU, and had really looked forward to being able to hang out with him. He was the oldest grandson in our extended family, and I'm the oldest granddaughter. While we had grown up in different states, I was (and still am) very close to his family. His death rocked our family. It was one of the defining moments of my life when it came to faith and eternal perspectives.

I got in the car and drove home, listening to Cactus Jack sing hymns, and pondering what had just happened.

The following Saturday, I went to visit Heather for an energy session to prepare for our upcoming expedition. We had 15 people on the trip, and I was a bit nervous after the challenges of the previous year.

One of the things that came out of the session that was really significant, was that we needed to create in Kenya a "Sacred Ecosystem" that included the environment and the people.

Often in this work, I've received messages that didn't make sense until later, and this was definitely one of them. I've just learned to be patient, and let God prevail. Sometimes, he just lets me be uncomfortable so that I can see His hand.

Heather told me that she wanted to come over the following Tuesday, the day before my flight, just for a refresh, so I agreed. While Heather and I don't share the same faith, we have a deep connection and understanding of each other. That's what happens when you share a mud hut in the hills of the Mara.

On Monday, May 29, 2017 I received a message from Moses when I woke up.

"Dad's gone."

Before I responded, I bowed my head and said a prayer. For the family, and for my own strength. I felt a deep peace, and immediately felt his dad's arms around me.

The next 24 hours were a blur as I tried to navigate the grief I felt, along with packing to get ready to fly to Kenya. The team was flying in Friday night very late. The funeral was on Saturday morning, and I would need to leave at 6:00 am to get there in time. My daughter, now 11, was coming with me to Kenya, and I didn't want to take her with me to the funeral. Leaving her in Nairobi with the team was daunting, but I knew that she would be in good hands.

It was Tuesday afternoon, and Heather messaged me and said, "I'm not going to get over there. Here's what I need you to do. I need Dave and the closest Priesthood holder going on the trip to give you a blessing. Then let me know what the blessing says. There's a message for you, but that needs to happen first."

About three weeks earlier, my neighbor Juan and his wife Patti had decided to join the trip. Otherwise, the closest Priesthood holder going on the trip was over an hour away. I thought her request was odd, but if there is one thing I have learned in all of this, it's just to follow those promptings.

That evening, Dave and I went over to Juan's house. In the blessing I was told that it wasn't a coincidence that he had passed away when he did, and that he wanted me to be at the funeral. While it was surprising to hear that in a blessing, it wasn't a huge surprise.

I got home and told Heather what had been said in the blessing.

"Nope, that's not it. That's obvious. What else?" she demanded.

"Uh, the team will be supportive and everything will go well?" I guessed.

"No, " she said.

A few minutes later she messaged me and said, "All is well." That's what the message is. I don't know what it means or who it is from. That's just what I am supposed to tell you. All is well. I'm sorry I don't have more."

While she was apologizing, my jaw was hitting the floor and my mind flashed back 27 years to the summer after my senior year of high school.

Chapter Twenty

July 14, 1990
Mark Earl Brotherson

I had just ordered pizza with my best friends Sara and Michelle, when I felt an overwhelming impression to go home. We had graduated from high school a few weeks earlier, and this was one of the last times we would be able to hang out before going our separate ways for college.

It was around 11:00 pm. On the drive home I vividly remember listening to the song "One" by Metallica. I wasn't into heavy metal, so I'm not sure why that song was on.

I walked in the house and the phone was ringing. This was back when phones were mostly attached to the wall, and no one ever called after 9:00 pm.

"Hi, Heidi, it's Aunt Donna. Is your mom there?"

I handed my mom the phone, and soon after heard her gasp. Their sister Karen had hit a deer on the way home from a family reunion. She had Mark and Jeanne with her. Jeanne had been life-flighted to Salt Lake. Mark had been thrown from the car and immediately killed.

Even as I write this 30 years later, I can't stop the tears when I think of that moment.

I spent much of the night helping my mom get ready to fly up to Salt Lake. The plan was for me to drive up with my Uncle David and Aunt Martha for the funeral. My cousin Eric was flying home from his mission for The Church of Jesus Christ of Latter-Day Saints in Alabama.

That morning at 7:00 am, I drove to a gas station in not-so-safe Central Phoenix where I had been working for the summer and saving for college. I needed to explain that I would be gone for a week. I pulled into the parking lot, and a car pulled in behind me. It was my dear friend and ecclesiastical leader, Lynn Hatch, wondering why I was at a gas station at 7:00 am on a Sunday morning.

I explained to him what happened, and he asked when my mom would be leaving for the airport. Lynn had been a father figure since I was seven years old. My mom was a single mom, and his family had adopted us and taken care of us throughout the years. His son Bret was one month and 26 days younger than me (and I rarely let him forget that) and we had been great friends for a decade.

I sent my mom off to the airport, closed the door, and broke down into sobs. I had mostly held it all in to be strong for her, but once I was alone, I couldn't hold back.

There was a knock on the door, and Lynn stood there with a piece of paper in his hand. Sundays are always the busiest days for leaders in my church, so I was surprised to see him standing there. I invited him in, and he handed me the piece of paper. It was a photocopy of a hymn in my church called "Come, Come Ye Saints."

He had hi-lighted the final verse:

And should we die before our journey's through
Happy day! **All is well!**
We then are free from toil and sorrow, too
With the just we shall dwell!

All is well.

Mark had answered my question. I had never told anyone that for almost 30 years, every time I sang the song, Mark had come to my mind. I think of it as my "Mark song." I hadn't told a single member of my family. Only Mark could have known that.

Miracle.

Chapter Twenty-one

June 1 – 13, 2017
8th Expedition to Kenya

After sharing with my friend, Heather, my story about Mark, and the fact that the message she shared with me came from the hymn that had made me think of Mark every time I heard it for 27 years, I got in a plane with my daughter to go back to Kenya for my 8th expedition.

Armed with the knowledge that indeed, Mark was helping me in Kenya, I had a renewed confidence in my ability to serve and lead a team.

That really was the best team, ever.

David, Tessa, Clara and Abbey at Bondeni School

I took Abbey and Tessa with me in the advanced team, and we went a day early to host a Days for Girls workshop at Bondeni School in Kayole, an area near Nairobi where Christine lived. We visited Christine's house to see where her team sewed the kits.

That Saturday morning I woke up at 5:00 am and hugged and kissed my daughter. I prayed fervently that everything would go well, and that we would all be safe. I then got in the car with my friend Mike, who would chauffer us to the funeral.

I had met Mike a couple of years earlier, when he drove us around Narok so we wouldn't have to take the jeep everywhere. It was nice to be able to drive with someone I knew, and when we stopped in Narok to pick up Moses's wife and daughters, I was able to meet his family as well.

"I want to drive," I said to Junior, Mike's younger brother.

The road to the Mara was rocky and unpaved at that time. We called it the African Massage. It was truly the worst road ever. Cars and jeeps broke down all the time, and there were often accidents.

For some reason, Junior agreed, and I drove from Noswani to Nkoilale, which was about 45 minutes back then. I pulled up alongside the tent where the funeral was to be held, and got out of the car.

I was the only white person there.

Shantel and Me

David Sasine, a friend of Moses and David, came to greet me and took me to Mama Helen's house. It was dark and full of people who were grieving, and the very last thing I wanted to do was make any sort of a scene.

Mama Helen was sitting on the couch, and her head was in her hand as she quietly cried. I reached down to take her other hand, knowing that she would know who I was as soon as she saw my skin color.

She erupted in fresh tears and shoved everyone aside to have me sit down next to her, where she threw her arms around me and told me she loved me. So much for not making a scene. I held my Maasai mom and cried with her. I felt out of place, inadequate, and I had absolutely no clue what a Maasai funeral was going to be like.

Turns out, not that different. Just goat and bread instead of ham and potatoes.

I sat down under the tent, and said to my friend Grace, "Just don't let me make a fool out of myself." She agreed that she would let me know of anything in advance.

Soon after, the hearse arrived and everyone began gathering. I was sitting in the back, trying to stay out of the way and be as inconspicuous as possible. The service was entirely in Maasai, so I didn't understand anything that was being said, until I heard my name.

"You're going to be asked to speak, "Grace said. "Go up there."

Whaaaaat?

Moses hadn't said anything about speaking. There were HUNDREDS of Maasai for me to walk through on my way to where my friend JJ was conducting.

JJ had actually been the warrior to give me my Maasai name on my first trip. He had wanted to name me something else, but Moses protested and told him what he wanted my name to be.

I turned to face the crowd and asked JJ to interpret for me.

I remember two things that I said. "The Masoi family has been my family since I first came to Kenya. I know my Maasai father is with God."

I walked back to my chair feeling humbled and in awe of what just happened. I later realized that I was the only woman who spoke at the funeral. When I sat down, Grace handed me a program.

On the cover was a picture I had taken of my Maasai father the year before. On the back was a picture of him with Mama Helen. That was the only picture ever taken of the two of them.

As I read through the program, I wondered why it was in English, when everyone there spoke Maasai. His biography and family history was written out. I felt his hand on my shoulder and felt him say, "This is why I needed you here."

What is the power of 100 people working together on any project in the world to create positive change? It starts with the one.

Let me take you back a bit to my first expedition in March of 2015, and my experience in the church at Eshemuli. I was taking a picture, remember? That picture was of Moses.

He had been sitting beside me, when I turned to him and said, "Smile!"

As I brought the camera down, I couldn't wrap my mind around what had happened. When I say, "the veil dropped," that's what I mean. I knew him. I KNEW him. I had just met him the day before, but it was like God was saying, "Everything that you have done in your life has led to this moment."

Let's just say Moses didn't have the same experience when I took that picture. In fact, I was just someone on the trip that he needed to be nice to. Hospitality, and all that. I made very little impression on him. After that experience, I felt the same connection with every Kenyan on our team.

Looking back, Moses, David, and Christine must have thought I was just crazy. They probably still think that, but they understand me a bit better now.

After the funeral, I worried how Moses was going to handle going right into an expedition with a huge team while he was in mourning. I was taken back to the hotel that night in Suswa to meet up with the group. The next morning Moses came in for breakfast and started leading. I was amazed at his strength, but I always am.

Olenkai is the nickname that Moses and David use for each other, and it means "Man of God."

The first thing that Moses did was gather the team to pray together in gratitude that we had all arrived safely. Then, we headed to Pastor Ben's church for services.

It was cold up in The Mau that day.

Christine, David, Moses and Me – My Family

On the agenda for the trip was building 15 garden boxes and fences for families between Suswa and the Mara. It was a lot of work ahead of us. We headed to our first family that afternoon.

Team Fence: Brent, Juan, Moses, David, Tessa, Chris & Abbey

We split into teams. Team Garden and Team Fence. That night I facilitated a fun personality test and talked about how they all work together. Team Fence largely consisted of warriors, and Team Garden consisted of everyone else. Wendy and I mostly talked and took pictures.

We had so much fun. I think it made it a little easier for Moses that the team was so amazing. We all took care of each other in unique ways that haven't happened in the same way since.

One day we were building Elizabeth's garden boxes, and we turned on music and started dancing. Juan and Patti led us all with Latin dancing and the Maasai were laughing at all of us. Part of what makes these experiences so great is the cultural immersion that takes place. We learn from each other.

My daughter and I were staying a few days extra on that trip to celebrate baby Heidi's first birthday. It was hard to say goodbye to the team. I didn't want it to end.

We dropped them off and headed back to the Mara. The jeep broke down and spent the next two days with its guts spilled all over the ground as it was being fixed.

Through all of that, Moses was a rock. A leader. A man of God.

It was time to celebrate some birthday.

Heidi didn't like me much back then. She occasionally let me hold her, but she was usually asleep when that happened, which was definitely to my advantage. She was beautiful, with fat, kissable cheeks.

I felt it was really important to be at her first birthday party. Her birthday is three days after Moses's, so first we surprised him with a party at Keekorok, a safari camp not far beyond the Sekenani Gate.

I had never been to a Maasai birthday party, either. Cake isn't eaten, it's thrown and smeared. The evening ended with Moses, David, and John completely covered in frosting. My daughter was instrumental in making sure that I didn't get covered as well.

At one point, while driving to the party, I looked at my daughter and said, "I'm not sure how we got here." There were three Maasai warriors in the front of the jeep, and three in the back. I'm a middle aged mom from Utah.

I've had a lot of moments like that over the years in which I've wondered why I was so blessed to do this.

Soon after my first trip to Kenya I had a dream during which my cousin Camie came to me. She had passed away a few years earlier, but had been a humanitarian who worked all over the world. At her funeral, her family shared that they had counted the stamps in her passport and she had gone to more than 90 countries.

During the dream, I asked her what I was supposed to do.

"I went wide. You're going deep. This is your tribe and your people."

My people.

Chapter Twenty-two

July 2017
Humanijam

I've always loved the music from the animated version of The Prince of Egypt. In fact, I really just love music. One day I was pondering and listening to the soundtrack when The Voice whispered, "He needs to leave his tribe to lead his tribe."

Considering I was listening to music from a soundtrack to a movie that was the story of Moses, I knew right away what to do.

A few weeks earlier, I attended Crowd Funding for Social Good, a workshop put on by my good friend Devin Thorpe. During the workshop, he recommended doing something "big" that would create awareness around the organization. I'm all for going big, as you have probably figured out by now!

I had decided to put on a different event and call it Humanijam as a tribute to Earl Jam, a family concert that my aunt and uncle put on annually. I messaged Moses and asked if he wanted to come for a couple of months and we would see if Lemarti could come for the concert. My hope was that he would be able to stay long enough to be mentored by different people we knew.

He agreed, and we booked the flight for September. We had big plans, including going to Disneyland. Okay, I had big plans. I sort of failed to tell Moses what they were.

When I'm in Kenya, I'm a bit more go-with-the-flow than I am in the U.S. Here, I'm an entrepreneur and networker and connector. And Moses the Maasai warrior was in the position of being dragged around to weekly meetings and lunches.

Mostly with middle-aged women.

"Don't you know any men?" He asked. Well yeah, I did, but I didn't hang out with them much.

We did some fun things with people who had gone with us to Kenya on previous trips. Lemarti was going to be flying in for the event about ten days early, and we were going to go to Disneyland for a few days.

That fell apart when Lemarti's wife went into labor and lost their baby daughter the night before he was supposed to come. It was devastating and awful.

I asked/persuaded my friend Jennifer to come with us to Disneyland. Moses was miserable. We met up with our friends Brian and June. June had been on the Best Team Ever trip with us.

In retrospect, it would have been fun to be there with Lemarti or David, who still hadn't been able to get his visa. While Moses never mentioned it, I think he was really grieving over his dad's death on that trip. He's used to being busy and having freedom and hanging out with warriors—not chatty female Americans.

I decided to get revenge on his crankiness by taking him on Guardians of the Galaxy. If you haven't been on it, it's the new version of Tower of Terror. It's dark, and you are in an elevator, and there are a lot of drops. If you don't know what you are in for, it's terrifying.

Moses had no idea.

"Are you going to tell him about the ride?" Brian asked as we waited just outside the doors to go in and get seated.

I looked at Brian with a smirk, and then turned to Moses and said, "There's kind of a drop on this ride." He ignored me.

We sat in our seats and I suggested that he put his hat and sunglasses away, or they would fly up to the ceiling. He ignored me, again.

Finally, I suggested that he hold on to the metal bars next to the seats. "I'll be fine," he said.

The ride started, and when the first drop hit, I had tears running down my face with laughter, as Moses wrapped his arms around me like a monkey and screamed, "When's it going to stooooooppppppppp?!"

Just as he didn't know that I could make horrific sounds when I cry, I didn't know he could scream like that.

He's going to kill me for including this story, but it was truly one of the most hilarious moments of my life. In fact, he has a whole arsenal of really horrible pictures of me on his phone that he is just waiting to unleash to the world. Telling this story might be what triggers that. I'll take the heat. It was awesome. Sometimes when I tell the story he even smiles a little.

I'm not sure we will ever get him to Disneyland, again, and definitely not on that ride!

The night of Humanijam came and I had asked Katie Jo to do a drum circle to close the night. We held it at an outdoor amphitheater and it was just a little too cold.

The next day, Moses was done, and we ended up in a wicked argument over the weekend. It was too long of a stay, and the plans for everything had fallen apart over and over again. He still had three weeks before flying home, and then a few days later I would be bringing a team. I was terrified.

That was really one of the worst days. Finally, I decided the best thing to do was to change his flight and pray that things would calm down. When you think about the fact that Moses and I are so different – ages, genders, continents, countries, languages – it's a miracle any of this happened. Communication between us is something we always have to work on.

The next day I messaged him and let him know his flight was changed to two days later. We were in the same house, not talking to each other.

"Do you have plans tonight, or can we do something before you leave?" I said the next day.

I had looked at what was playing at our local theater, thinking that maybe a movie would be neutral. I invited Vilia to join us, an experience that was super fun for her considering the tension. We went to eat first, and as we sat at the table, Moses pulled out a piece of paper. He fidgeted a bit, and then said, "This is the estimate for the guest house from the contractor."

I was very cautious, and took the piece of paper. Twenty-four hours earlier I thought that this all was over. The conversation was all business, but it gave me a bit of hope.

The movie I chose was a movie that was playing for only three days. It was a documentary called "Mully" about a man in Kenya who had been a street boy and worked his way up to being a millionaire before shutting it all down in order to rescue orphan children.

In the movie, they talked about how the Mullys had planted millions of trees, and changed the ecosystem in a very dry area of Kenya. I was mesmerized. That sacred ecosystem that Heather had talked to me about a few months earlier flooded my mind.

At the end of the movie, I leaned forward in my seat, and without looking at Moses said, "Can we do this?"

"Yeah," he said.

I think we both knew at that time, that we were stuck with each other. I always tell people who come with me to find their ONE. The one person that they are meant to connect with to create change. Moses has always been that person for me.

Chapter Twenty-three

November 1 – 14, 2017
9th Expedition to Kenya

On March 3, 2015, two days before I left for Kenya for the first time, I launched a book called Homeschool on Fire: Be the CEO of Your Business and Homeschool. It went #1 on Amazon two days before I got on a plane to go to Kenya for the first time. It's pretty easy to hit #1 on Amazon in the homeschool category when you launch a book on a Tuesday.

Because of that, I was often getting asked to speak at homeschool conferences.

A tiny dark-haired woman with lots of curls sneaked into the back of the room and I immediately knew she would be going to Kenya with me. Then she sneaked out before I was finished, so I wondered why I had thought that.

A little while later, she came over to my table at the conference with her daughter.

"We want to go to Kenya," she said. I smiled.

We exchanged information, and the following year she came with me in June 2016 when we went to Bomet for the first time.

A few weeks prior to leaving, we had been sitting in my living room and I said, "I don't think Bomet is mine. I think it's yours."

She hadn't been to Kenya, and here I was telling her that she was going to have stewardship over a place I hadn't been, either. No, that's not weird at all.

Jenn, being the pondering type, just nodded a bit. But I was right. She immediately bonded with Anita in Bomet, and felt pulled to work there from then on.

February 2017, she came to me and said she felt her family needed to move to Kenya to work for a while. She didn't know how long, but wanted my input on what that would look like. We coordinated with Anita, who was able to have Jenn and her family stay in her house in Litein, about 45 minutes from Bomet.

About a week before the June 2017 trip, her family moved to Kenya.

I hadn't been back to Bomet since our first trip, and there was tension there with my Kenya team. Tribalism is a challenge there, and there was a lot of misunderstanding.

What I didn't know, and am so grateful for, was that Jenn would create bridges and help heal all of that.

"Landed," I texted to Moses and David when we had cell service again.

"Waiting," David replied.

"I'm not there," Moses said, "I'm stuck in a jam at the Escarpment. Kaelo will pick you up."

I have a recurring nightmare, literally, that I will arrive in Nairobi and no one will be there. This was just a few weeks after sending Moses home early, and we had been on shaky ground, although Moses had told me that there was nothing to worry about.

The next day, we went to the Giraffe Centre, always a favorite for our expedition teams. It was a special group. I had Becky and Bridget with me, two of the friends who had stuck with me through all of the drama. I also had Abbey and Lori, who had been with me a few months before on The Best Team Ever trip.

Finally, Moses met up with us at the Giraffe Centre and I could breathe a sigh of relief. As he walked up, he laughed and said, "I bet you were worried."

Building a Water Storage System at Pastor Ben's

Our big objectives for the trip were to build three water storage systems with huge tanks attached to houses to capture rainwater. We had four men on that trip, plus Jenn's husband Forrest.

November is usually warm and sunny, but that year it was cooler with a lot of rain. The previous year when we wanted to plant trees it had been dry and dusty. People ask me what the weather is like during a particular time of year and I always laugh. I've never had the same type of weather twice.

Our first stop was visiting the Oiboo family to see how things were going with their garden. Since Abbey and Lori had been there when we built it, we were all really excited to see if it had grown.

We arrived at their house, and got out of the jeep.

Chapter Twenty-three

Abbey and Lori See the Oiboo's Garden

As we came up to the garden, we all burst into tears. Not only had the garden grown, but they had taken the initiative to expand it! They told us that they were feeding their family (with 16 kids) and that they were able to help support extended family with school fees, because they weren't spending money on as much food. It had worked!

Our excitement followed us to Pastor Ben's church where we joined in the worship and then visited families in his congregation afterward. Two girls who were adorable and sang for us captured our hearts. They were struggling with school fees, and without electricity at night were unable to study. We decided that they would be the next students we sponsored.

Typically when we are working in an area we identify students that we can support, and be able to work a bit with their families in self-reliance projects. Agnes and Nashipae's father had abandoned the family, leaving two wives and several children. They live in a remote area of the Mau Forest, where resources are scarce.

Agnes and Nashipae

When we ask families what their biggest challenges are, it's most often access to food, water and help with school fees. We can't help every family, but when certain children come across our path and we are inspired to help, we help.

On that trip, Jenn and her husband and four kids joined us, so our team was pretty big, and we were able to get a lot done. We wrapped up our projects in Suswa, and headed to Narok, where we were going to a new community called Nkareta.

On our way out, we stopped at the lumber yard to get more wood for a garden box for the Mara, and Jenn said, "Heidi, please ask Moses if you could come with me this afternoon to Bomet. They really need to see you. I know it's a big ask, but please ask."

I didn't know what to say. We were going to get to Narok early, so we had plenty of time to run up to Bomet for a few hours, but it was a huge conflict. I decided to ask David what he thought.

The look on his face let me know that there was no way it would happen. "Let's talk to Moses," he said. A few minutes later, Moses got in the jeep and said, "David tells me you want to go to Bomet with Jenn. By yourself, or with other people?"

I braced myself and said, "Becky, Bridget, and Lori."

Moses is hard to read, and he was quiet for a few moments before he said, "You can go."

I knew it was a big deal. They take our security very seriously in Kenya, and it's not often that I'm not with either Moses or David doing anything. I knew I had better head out before he changed his mind.

We got in Jenn's car and started on the road to Bomet. It was my first time in a car in Kenya without any Kenyans, and I've got to say, we had a really fun drive. It was still rainy when we arrived in Bomet, where we met up at the sewing center.

Visiting Bomet

Anita was living in Mombasa at the time, so she wasn't there, but we saw her mom, Nancy, and Mercy and Vincent. Vincent was one of the students we had agreed to sponsor in school, and he was in his final year.

Mercy was one of our success stories. When we met her, she had been working for $1/day cutting vegetables in a field. After receiving a cow, goat, and chickens, she was able to sell milk and eggs. She was also learning how to sew the reusable feminine hygiene kits. We visited her house, and got caught up with Vincent.

Nancy explained that the support we had given Mercy had helped her overcome depression. She said, "She wasn't right up here," and pointed to her head. Her family was still struggling, but she felt hope. Not to reveal too much about book two, but Mercy and Vincent play a huge role.

Mercy's Family

There were so many people we wanted to visit, but time ran short, and the muddy roads were impassable from the rain. We started heading back and I was getting frustrated texts from Moses saying, "Where are you?!"

We arrived safely back at the hotel, and I felt sadness, wondering if I would be able to go back. I really loved that community, I was committed to the Maasai, but I felt peace there. I felt God there.

A few days earlier, our team had decided to go on a little adventure, and we drove up Mount Suswa with the goal of visiting caves that are special to the Maasai.

As we climbed the mountain in the jeep, our guide was explaining in Maasai about the history, with Moses interpreting. At one point he pointed and said, "That's where the Maasai prophet and his family lives."

I had never heard of this. There was a Maasai prophet? I knew that they didn't have a Christ figure in their traditional belief. They believed in one God, Enkai, but Christianity had come only in the past 30 years.

Mount Suswa means Mountain of God, and as we drove I was amazed at the beauty of the land. We weren't able to get to the caves before dark, but we stopped and took pictures, and learned that there is a place that only the Maasai prophet goes. This is where Maasai will go to pray special prayers.

David, Moses, Muneria and Me on Mount Suswa

In February 2019, Scott and Becky Mackintosh led a team to Kenya and went back to the caves. When they got home from their trip, Becky messaged me that she had a gift for me from

Moses. It was a beautiful piece of obsidian from the cave, and as I type, it sits next to me. Often when I am working something out in my mind, I grab the rock and use it as a worry stone.

As we drove on the extremely bumpy and rut-filled road to Nkareta, I felt we were going back in time. While it was not far away from Narok, it was a place that time forgot. Our plan was to meet two families – The Peres and Kirimogos – and do assessments on what they needed, and how we could help them.

Moses had talked about working with Jacob for quite a while, and finally I got to meet him.

The Pere Family

It was a major turning point in our work in Kenya. Jacob was a community director in Nkareta, much respected by the people of the community. From the first, I was impressed with his leadership and his desire to better the lives of his people. I'm actually amazed that Moses allowed us to get to know each other, because when we start planning, we rapid-fire ideas. It's hilarious.

Nkareta was like Bomet. It was an area where we could go deep and make a big impact, but I didn't really know that at the time. The community was all Maasai, and it was still in The Mau, but a different area from where we had worked before.

A few wonderful connections came from that day, and we were excited to see what we could do there.

The next day, David told us that he had arranged for us to visit a rescue center run by his first schoolteacher. It was hidden right in Narok, with over 60 girls who had run from Female Genital Mutilation (FGM) and early marriage. I was excited to meet the girls and learn their stories. We had Christine with us, so she quickly organized a workshop to donate reusable feminine hygiene kits.

The girls were beautiful. We decided to take on four of the girls to sponsor in school, which was a big challenge for us financially, but our budget has never matched our dream—it's matched our faith.

One of the wonderful experiences we had at the rescue center was creating connections with the girls. They started off a bit shy, but by the end were singing, dancing, and hugging us.

Distributing Kits at the Rescue Centre

At last, we headed to the Mara, where two of our students, Fred and Ndee, joined us for a few days to help our team. During November and December, all of Kenya is out of school and the students are on holiday.

Fred and Ndee

We took them with us to build garden boxes and the water tower systems. It was fun to have them along and get to know them. We try not to sponsor students unless we meet them first, and it's become important to us that when possible, we give them an opportunity to work with us for a few days.

This was so early in our journey sponsoring students. I can't wait to share with you in Book Two, *Feed My Sheep*, what has happened to our students and where they are going in life. They're like my kids. Truly.

At the cultural centre, we had built a small guard house out of iron sheets, the only structure on the land. We decided to have an official ribbon cutting ceremony, which ended up just being hilarious, because we didn't have ribbon. One of our team members loved to crochet, so she made us a yarn strip that we cut with a machete.

It was official. We had a building.

The Original Guard House

Chapter Twenty-four

January 2018
The Underwear Story

One day, I got a call from the news. We had been nominated by our friend Becci Webb to receive the Mountain America Pay it Forward award, and had been chosen to be interviewed about one of our projects. Since most of our projects were in Kenya, we chose one that we had been talking about launching.

I met Marissa in a business mastermind seminar run by our mutual coach in Australia. We had gotten to know each other, and I invited her to join me in Kenya. She set a plan to go in June 2018, having never had a passport before. Marissa is a professional seamstress, and asked me if I could think of a pattern she could create for Kenya.

"Underwear," I said, almost right away.

I thought about Christine's story for the book *Success through Failure*, and how her underwear was so full of holes that even if she had been able to get menstrual pads, she didn't have a way to use them.

"Underwear that they can make that doesn't require elastic," I added.

Marissa got to work, and within a day or two had a three-piece pattern that would work. We realized that we could use donated t-shirts for the fabric, and got to work trying it out.

Okay, she got to work. I am really great at cutting out the patterns, but sewing has continued to be something that I don't personally do. I leave it to the experts.

We decided that for the Pay it Forward segment, we would host a sew-a-thon, and make underwear to take to the rescue center we had visited in November. We gathered together at a library and after several hours, we had produced 67 pair of underwear.

In addition, Mountain America donated $500 to us, so we were able to get 50 reusable feminine hygiene kits as well. It was a cool experience, and kicked off a year of sew-a-thons and hundreds of pairs of underwear.

We took the pattern to Kenya, where we taught Christine and Anita and their teams to make them. Marissa even had the opportunity in 2019 to teach over 100 girls at a girls camp how to hand sew them.

It's funny how something so simple becomes so meaningful and opens doors.

A few nights later, I had a scheduled call with Moses to discuss the upcoming March trip. I mentioned to him that Jenn's parents were coming, and would probably go to Bomet for a few days to spend time with their grandchildren. What he said next made my jaw hit the floor.

"Jenn has done a really great job. I think that we should go to Bomet for a few days."

I was speechless for a moment. And then I launched into full question mode. As soon as I got off the phone, I messaged Jenn that the team was coming to Bomet. She was ecstatic.

Jenn and Anita had been discussing for two years the need to build a training center. The sewing center was dark and cramped, and they needed space for literacy classes and other training that was needed. With a team coming, she knew she would have help with building, so she went to work planning and organizing the fundraising.

It would be a brick building, next to the sewing center. A lot of pre-work needed to be done to get ready for us to arrive. I let Jenn know that it was her job to plan the three days we would be there, and to keep me updated on what was needed.

Then things just got weird, and the opposition hit hard. People weren't signing up, or they were signing up and then dropping out. Jenn's parents had recruited two of their St. George friends, but leading up to about three weeks before the trip, we had only ten people going.

Too many for one jeep, and too few for two jeeps. I've got to admit, I was getting a bit stressed.

Then one day, I got three messages in one day. The first was from my friend Shelley, who said that she and her husband wanted to join us on the trip.

The second message came from Debra, who told me she had been to Africa twice, and had heard about our organization. She wanted to know when we were going next and I said, "June. Well, actually next week, but the next trip is in June."

"Do you have room next week?" she asked.

The third message came from Stephen Story asking if there was a spot for him. That made 14. We were ready to roll.

Chapter Twenty-five

March 15 – 25, 2018
10th Expedition to Kenya
100 People

The makeup of the teams is always entertaining, because the people who come with us come from all walks of life. The March 2018 group was especially eclectic. One-third of the team had been to Kenya before, one-third had tattoo sleeves, and one-third were temple workers in the St. George temple for The Church of Jesus Christ of Latter-Day Saints. It was closed for cleaning that week.

One thing that I have always said about our trips, is that it is a melting pot of backgrounds. We are there to serve and have whatever experience we are meant to have. Sometimes a group really clicks, and sometimes they don't. I was really curious what would happen with such a mix.

We started off the trip with a side jaunt to Naivasha, where Jenn's son was baptized, before heading down to Narok. The rain was unbelievable. It was so bad that if we had walked out from under the building eaves, we would have been drenched immediately. A river was running down the road and there was nowhere to step. The jeeps couldn't reach us.

A couple of months earlier, Moses had said that rain was needed in Kenya, so I told him I would pray for that. A few minutes later it started raining, so he dubbed me the "Rainmaker."

That day he said we needed to change that to "Rainstopper," because once it had started raining, it had not stopped. Flooding was happening all over Kenya, and there was even a giant crack in the road to Narok that kept reopening every few days.

We were dramatically delayed and arrived at our hotel after dark, soaked and hungry. We had a long drive the next day to get to Bomet, plus a few days of building and training families.

After a night with not much sleep due to a local nightclub playing music at top volume (we don't stay at that hotel anymore) we got on the road and arrived in Bomet in time to host a Days for Girls workshop at a school called Siwot. We almost got stuck on the road to get there because of the rain, but it was so worth it!

Days for Girls Workshop

The only problem was, the Days for Girls kits were in the back of a truck carrying our luggage, to the hotel. Oops.

We spent some time standing around until we could get started with the girls, and finally a boda boda arrived with the kits.

The men went in with the boys at the school to teach a workshop as well. I wasn't there, but I heard it was pretty powerful. It was the first time that we had a boys workshop at the same time.

The girls were curious, and the room was crowded and muggy from all of the rain. The floor was streaked with mud, and our team just added to the mess with our boots.

Christine had joined us on the trip, and since Anita wouldn't arrive until the next day, she led the workshop. This was Kalenjin country. The language was different, and the girls understood a little bit of English and a little more Swahili.

Each member of the team played a part, from showing the girls how to wash their hands for better hygiene, to Debra standing on a chair and demonstrating how to snap the kit onto underwear. That's always the part where girls erupt into embarrassed giggles.

Tears of happiness leaked out of my eyes a few moments after we handed out the kits, when Jenn led the girls in a shout of "I am happy! I am strong! I am smart! I am kind! I am important! I am a CHILD OF GOD!"

How do I even explain what goes through my head and heart in these moments? It's like Heaven and Earth meet, the veil parts, and I get a glimpse of what this life is really all about.

Building the Bomet Training Center

The next day, we began building our first training center in Kenya in a torrential downpour, which ironically made mixing cement a lot easier for us. We knew we wouldn't be able to finish the training center during our visit, but the foundation was laid, so that the construction team could continue after we were gone.

Paul and Me

The next day we headed out to visit families and build a garden box with Paul. Paul had been helping to build some of the garden boxes in the area, and would never accept help for himself, even though he needed it.

First, we went to visit Janet. On our first trip to Bomet, we had met Ivyn, whose parents had HIV. Her mother had left the family because of the stigma, and Ivyn and her siblings were left with their alcoholic father. We sponsored Ivyn in school so that she wouldn't be married off, as she had reached the age of 15 and was considered an adult in the community.

Ivyn's father had passed away, and her mother, Janet, returned to the home. Sadly, she was diagnosed with cancer shortly afterward. To help Ivyn's family, we provided a garden box and a goat for nutrition.

Donating a Goat to Janet

There were a few families that were receiving chickens to start a project that would allow them to sell eggs to make an income. Anita and Jenn had done an incredible job with vetting families and training them in advance, making our job easier.

We finally headed to Paul's house, where we had a really fun day. We turned on music and started dancing, which attracted other members of the community who were interested in what we were doing. Paul was all smiles and thumbs up. The rest of us were covered in dirt.

As often as possible, we love to bring in the community to learn about what we are doing. It's how we are able to expand our projects so quickly. We've found that Kenyans are incredibly giving, and love to share what they learn with their neighbors.

Jenn, David, Christine, Moses and Me

Our final day in Bomet, we headed back to the training center after building more garden boxes and donating more chickens and goats. The three days in Bomet were amazing and it was so great to see the families again that we had worked with two years earlier. They had progressed a great deal and we saw that miracles had been happening.

Moses Speaking to the Group

A lot of healing took place over those few days, and I was really grateful to be able to go back and bring the team. Although we had to slog through mud, it was worth it.

We ended the day with a break in the rain under a soggy tent next to the training center. We all gathered and shared what it meant to be together again. Each person had the opportunity to share something, and at the end, Anita whispered to me, "Should we finish with a prayer?"

"Ask Moses to give it, "I replied.

He gave a beautiful prayer. It was fitting to go back to Bomet, where so much began. I love the people there. I love the peace. But the Mara is home. I was grateful for that knowledge.

Chapter Twenty-five

Anita and Me

We were able to accomplish a great deal that trip. We visited the Rescue Centre, where we took suitcases full of underwear we had sewn for the girls, as well as supplies like toothpaste and toothbrushes. We visited two of the girls we had chosen to sponsor at their school, meeting them there for the first time.

Jacinta and Sereti were so cute when we met them. They started off a little shy, and then opened up and became really chatty about their lives and school. They were in their first year of high school, so everything was new for them. Both of them had been at risk of Female Genital Mutilation and early marriage before we agreed to sponsor them.

Jacinta and Sereti

It was time to head out to the Mara, where we would work on our next projects.

In November, we had built a water storage system at David's house, and had gotten a donation for water filters, so we wanted to test it out to see how it would work. I was a bit skeptical, but decided to try the water. I had no issues. It made me hope a bit for the future, and being able to bring filters instead of carrying around plastic water bottles everywhere we went.

Testing out the Water Filter

Our last day on the Mara we built a garden box for Moses's mom, Mama Helen. While we worked on it, Moses and Mama Helen cleared out underneath the Wisdom Tree, so that our team could have a picnic after we worked. At one point I looked over and saw them, and Jenn nudged me and said, "You should go pray with them."

I walked over and stood there for a few minutes watching them work. I was flooded with gratitude that I was somehow chosen to do this work, even though it was often challenging and emotional.

I asked Moses if we could pray under the Wisdom Tree, and the three of us held hands while Mama Helen prayed in Maasai. I have no idea what she said, and it doesn't matter. I'm just grateful that I experienced it.

Moses and Mama Helen Under the Wisdom Tree

What is the power of 100 people?

It took 10 expeditions to reach that tipping point. And indeed, it was a tipping point for what was to come, but those stories will be shared in the next book. For now, I hope that this answers the question, "How did you get started in Kenya?"

For those of you reading this who have a dream in their heart of doing something like this, my best advice is: Do it, but expect it to be a refiner's fire for you. Expect opposition. Expect to gain incredible friendships, and expect to lose people along the way who don't agree with your vision.

But most of all, expect miracles.

Utah

September 2019
Called by God

An Interview with Moses Masoi, preview to Book Two:
Feed My Sheep

This interview was transcribed from a video. The transcript has been kept in his voice.

Tell us a little bit about who you are.

My name is Moses Masoi. I come from Kenya. I am the Executive Director for 100 Humanitarians Kenyan Chapter and I spearhead the expeditions there and organize and supervise the projects that we have over there in Kenya.

And how long have you been doing this?

Roughly four years and counting.

Ok, you've seen a lot of changes take place in the communities we work in, in Kenya, over the past few years. What has made the biggest impression on you about how this is changing your community?

I think the biggest change that I can see coming to the community is the education of the students that we have in our educational program.

Education always is the catalyst of any positive change in any society, in any tribe, or anywhere in the world. I see that as a positive direction that these families are embracing and taking part of. Also, education includes the Training Center that we have for women.

We already have two functional training centers, one in Bomet and one in Nkareta. These adult training centers, where we are training women how to sew and other life skills that they would not have got, because most of them did not go to school. This is all part of education and education brings positive changes anywhere in the world.

So that is one of the biggest things that I see has been of great impact that can be really seen. Also the Business Boxes that we do. We've had families that started from earning zero income in a month and we are now seeing them earning on the level of up to $200 per month and some less depending on where they are, and some even more than that, with the chickens, the goats, the gardening towers and the cows we provided for them has brought a whole new chapter to their lives.

One that they did not have before and one that we are happy to say that they have been good custodians of the projects that we started for them. You can see the whole difference. The nutrition of the babies, how well dressed they are, how happy they are, and you can see the whole family radiates love and joy in them because of the project that has been put in their family.

So I think those three things have been some of those that have had the biggest impact on their family livelihoods and also not forgetting keeping girls in school through the provision of sanitary towels which has helped a lot in (inaudible) for school-going girls both in primary school and in high school. These have seen improved grades for girls and improved performance in both academic and extracurricular activities.

When we started four years ago, did you anticipate that this is how big it would have gotten? Is this what you saw happening?

Well, I am a visionary person and given the right resources I would have envisioned us farther than this. But the steps we've taken are way further than I expected with the little that we had and the little capacity we had money-wise and (inaudible)_ wise and have seen things that I did not anticipate could have happened at this time.

We have two active garden towers that are almost many families that we visit, fully built training centers for women that we are going to equip, many things - the schools that we have children in. We have almost four or five students graduating this year that we started from 8th grade and some from the first year of high school.

The general view of the families when we visit them, that we've provided Business Boxes to, is something that you don't have the right words to express how much this has been of immense change to them and also to the society that they live in.

I've seen women in Bomet do garden towers by themselves and then training others. Some women doing the same thing in Nkareta, taking the initiative of training others on how they doing these. Using the Hope Sacs to make their meals using less fuel, and also the performance of the students that we are sponsoring. We've seen gradual improvement.

We've had them fall with lower grades, because of the disappointments, knowing that they probably weren't going to finish school because of their financial issues, but since we were able to sponsor their education we've seen gradual improvement in their performance academically.

The further we've come when we started with Business Boxes, now we are at Garden Towers and now we have Training Centers, we have more kids than we have done before, we have more kids in school today. We have more families that have had a hand in one way or another, either through the chickens or goats or garden towers.

These are some of the things that I did not anticipate to have happened in such a short time of four years. But I see that this is just the beginning and I believe that the next years to come will see tremendous expansion in where we can reach because we intend to reach to other regions. Kiisi, and whichever regions that we can reach and offer a helping hand to needy families and children going to school and needy families in those societies.

So, 100 Humanitarians International likes to go into communities and help build the infrastructure and build a stewardship for that community and then we want to teach them self-reliance so we can move into mentoring and training versus setting up all of these systems and the Business Box for Families and things.

If you were to share your vision for what you want to have happen on the Maasai Mara, which is your community, what you want to see done over the next 3-5 years, what would that be?

Honestly speaking, we've done already things that have been in line with the visions and the objectives of this organization from the word go. We've been lucky enough to have very supportive people, both the donors from America and other parts of the world, and we've also had a very supportive Kenyan team that have gone out of their way to see this community change.

Something drives them to see these communities better and having a good life. Also we've had very wonderful reception from the communities that we've been working with. They have received us with joy and open hands. Whatever little we've been able to do for them they have received with pride and took them as theirs. I believe that this has been like a family working together. That is the most beautiful thing.

We don't work like strangers or tourists, we are like a family that are working together towards a common goal, which is seeing those families live a better life, seeing those children finish school, and perform well.

But of course I don't want to go into details of that. I really wish that we could finish up with the building of the Cultural Center on the Maasai Mara. It's one of the pillars and the foundation of everything we're building in Kenya because we want to be able to teach something new to the people but also preserving their culture and way of life. Not trying to erode them or wash away what they believe in and what they know.

But introducing alternative ways and ways of doing things better in a way that can enable them financially and socially to be better people and better versions of themsleves, which includes adult literacy and the Days for Girls, the (inaudible) program between girls and families that they were running away from early marriages and FGM, and also as a community meeting hub where all the social practices that were not being able to be performed right now because of the land implication and how the Maasai have been dispersed into private lands.

That we can all have a common place to call home, to come together to celebrate our heritage, our culture, and also to learn new ways. Of course it's the exchange of ideas, cultures, skills that people can learn from groups visiting and also they can teach the groups visiting stuff.

It's all to the goal of helping them to sustain themselves financially, to run the projects and to take that to the future generation and even to teach the families, when you get something make good use of it. Be able to learn and keep their skills and teach their neighbors so it can go forth to the community.

What do you see are the biggest challenges facing the Maasai today?

The Maasai, like any other community, are facing challenges which are brought about by development, Westernization, and the impact of tourism, both local and international tourism, and also the interaction with other tribes. I think the biggest thing that the Maasai are losing is their pride and the pride of the Maasai is involved in too many things, which I believe are the main things that identify someone as Maasai.

One is their culture that is gradually being eroded by education and interaction with other communities, industrialization, and the whole concept of being Westernized maybe. Gradually the Maasai are losing their way of living, the way they used to eat, their mode of dressing, their cultural practices. They are losing them.

They are adopting new cultures either from the neighboring tribes or from Western tribes that they watch on TV, that they read in magazines and that they can also learn from schools.

They're also picking up and keeping concepts they learn from religious practices like churches. So that's one of the things that I see is being lost in our Maasai area. The other thing the Maasai are losing is their cows. Any man in the Maasai community would take pride in having as many cows as he could possibly have. But with the demarcation of the land people have gotten very small portions of land that cannot sustain many cows that the Maasai took pride in having.

So right now they are limited to having very few cows and they can no longer use their land because most of the land has been preserved for conservancies and the other land is used for the national reserve which they are not allowed to graze their cows in anymore. So with that coming it's up to the Maasai to learn how to adapt to those changes, either to minimize the amount of cows they have, or learn to breed their cows, to have a better breed of cows that provide a higher yield of milk or even weight if it was to be sold to the market or to be used for food, and also to learn what aspects of the Maasai traditions to keep and what aspects of the Maasai culture traditions to let go as we focus into the future.

Those two things, I feel, are the biggest threat to the Maasai culture, to the Maasai tradition and the community itself.

With the building of the Cultural Center, what can we do to preserve that culture? What are the things we can do as part of the Cultural Center that will really make an impact and make a difference in making sure that the Maasai moving

forward have those opportunities, that your children and your grandchildren will know and understand what it means to be a Maasai because of this Cultural Center?

The way the world is going right now and the way forward is digital. I believe the only way we can do right now is collect as many stories as possible from the elders, to collect original Maasai artifacts, original Maasai things that you cannot find elsewhere, to record family ancestry, and put all those in an online portal that any Maasai anywhere in the world can access, and especially at the Cultural Center.

That during free time when kids need to learn about their tradition, their games that get played, the kind of stories that were being told about heroism, about legends, that they can still get that online. I've seen many people writing the same stories in books but let's face it. In the coming years everyone will want to read their book on the phone or the computer. That's where we are heading.

As we adapt to those changes, we must ensure that those changes have Us in them. That as the world moves into a digital era, the Maasai will be part of that digital era, with the stories told, with the artifacts there, and with their practices and traditions preserved in a way that children that will come 10 or 20 or 30 years to come, that the next generations can still retrieve this information, can still go back and know about them. I believe that there will come a time even in the future that there will be conflicts.

We've always had our own conflict resolution measures that we still practice today. And as much as their courts and their other legal measures of solving conflicts, to solve any Maasai conflicts, you always have to go back to the books and go back to the traditions like this is how this was being solved, this is how this matter is solved traditionally. I believe that there will come a time when someone will want to go back to the books, go back to the computer and search for these things, like, Hey I went back and I found out, this is what the Maasai used to do.

This is how we believe this can be solved. I believe that what I would really envision, what I would love to see even when I am dead and I am looking down on my great-grandchildren and other people living in our society that they can go to their new computers or whatever they are using at that time, and still be able to trace their heritage, trace their culture and trace their practices and be proud of them. Something that is still (inaudible) show them that they are Maasai and they believe in these practices and what they used to do, even if it's different right now.

How is your life different than your father's, in one generation?

Well, my life was not so different from my father's, but it was different in many aspects. I did not find the practice of cow raiding, where if you needed wealth you had to go to another community, kill someone, or kill a whole community to get your cows and sheep and goats. I think that's the only aspect I did not get of my parents, but all the other practices that were being practiced traditionally, I had to take part in most of them unless some that were not allowed because of going to school.

Those are things that my children would never experience or even generations a few years ago did not experience and would never experience. Which is a shame because I really wish that they went through those things. Those are things that cannot be narrated and cannot even be expressed fully in a book or in a digital format. Those are things that can only give you the pride if you went through them and you understood them. But it's the least we can do for our children and even great-grandchildren and the people that come after us, that even if you cannot experience this, this is how the Maasai lived.

I look forward to movies being created of the Maasai cultures, just like Disney did with the Lion King and they did the whole moderning, the thing that made it even more realistic and more lively. I look forward to maybe in the coming years, a whole thing can be created of the Maasai practices, the lion hunting, the raids and practices and can all be re-lived either using technology or whatever things will be used at that time.

That when someone watches them, they can actually almost feel like this is happening and this is how the real thing was being done. I did not experience everything that my parents did and my children will not experience everything that I did. But I try as much as possible to ensure that my kids learn that they are Maasai and the tribe and I take every opportunity that I am able to teach them a thing or few. I hope that in the future we can have a whole thing that they can go to and learn everything that they want to about Maasai.

The cultural center is called the Emparnat Cultural Center. What does the word "Emparnat" mean to you?

Emparnat in the Maasai tongue means a place where people can never move. It's like a living place that people never move out from. In the Maasai tradition we used to build temporary homes which we would live in for a certain period and then when grass got scarce and water was scarce too, we'd move to another area and so forth and so forth.

But then there came a time when people would build Emparnat, which is a village that they would live in for many years and they would only be moving from one spot to another in the same area like shifting houses since sometimes the houses get old, they get eaten by the termites and they start bending, so they just move to another area. Emparnat's a place where people live forever and that they love and the existence of the social life continues in that area for ages and ages.

The whole existence of the Emparnat Cultural Center is that as the Maasai people are living in different parts of the Maasai Mara, the Emparnat Cultural Center is there. They can always live there socially and they can always come there to relive their practices there, to do whatever competitions they want to do there and it's something that's there to stay even after I go, and many other people that will go after me, the Emparnat Cultural Center will be there to stay.

It will be for use of the community and the people living there for years and years and years to come.

What does this mission and purpose in building this cultural center, in doing this for your community, for your tribe, literally creating a legacy and a home where this culture can be preserved forever long after you are gone, what does that mean to you personally?

It means everything to me. In my own personal experience I feel like this is a path that was being prepared by God and God prepared me for this from a long time ago. And in so doing, he provided me with the right opportunities, made my paths collide with the right people with the same vision, with the same motivation of doing these things and this means everything to me.

It reminds me of the day that I quit my job and just did not know what I was going to do but I had this strong feeling that I was hoping for the right thing and ever since then I've always felt like everything I wanted to do was humanitarian.

I've always thought of the people more than I've thought of conservation for instance. I was a safari guide. I've thought of the people more than I thought of the animals and in any conflict that involved the people or the wildlife or the environment, I always thought of the people first.

If this really happens, and I know it's going to happen, it will be a fulfillment of a dream that I had. I always dreamed that I wanted a place where the Maasai can learn. That the women who are not able and lucky enough to go to school can still get to a point in life where they can learn any literacies that they want to learn.

They can learn any skills that they want to learn and they can learn to be carpenters, they can learn to sew, they can learn anything that they want to be. And the opportunities are unlimited to anyone. Even the Maasai boys and girls who were not able to go to college. I remember going to college I had to sell the last few cows that I had because none of my brothers supported me in that.

And I paid for my own fees until I was done, got myself a job, and I believe that this has been more of a calling and a way that God has been directing me, that this was what to do.

And he has provided opportunities that sometimes I'm like, "How did that happen?" And he's always had his own way of making things work and I believe that even if the cultural center is going to take 20 years or 30 years, whether I"ll be alive or not, I believe it's going to happen. It's going to fulfill God's own plan for the Maasai people, God's own plan for the people living there even if they're not Maasai.

Us getting that land was not coincidental. We've had people who lived in that area and they were moved when the land was still mud. They were moved far away from that place. There were other families who were way more deserving than ours was, moved to other areas, and we were lucky enough to get the place there in the right place where we needed it.

Also I think that having a family which I'm doing (inaudible) and my brothers and my parents both supported what I'm doing and they saw the need even if sometimes they were l/ike, "What are you doing?" And I was like, "I'm building a cultural center." And they were like, "How are you going to benefit from it?" And I'm like, "It's not about me. It's about what God wants to happen and what the people need in that place.

Personally, I look back to the four years that we've come. We started with very little hope in ourselves and very little in our capacity to do stuff that we wanted to do. And looking back and seeing what we've been able to achieve over the four years, the kind of people that God has brought to our paths both locally in Kenya and even here in the U.S.

When we started it was Heidi, me, probably with the same vision only. And over the years we've had people come in. We've had Jacob, Christine, Anita, David, John, and Other David. And also in the U.S. the community is expanding, the family is expanding and we have people that are l/ike, "What do you guys do?" And every time I'm driving people in the bus and they ask, "Are you a safari guide?" and I'm like, "No. I'm a humanitarian."

"What do you mean a humanitarian?" And I'm like, "I drive people to see the animals, but I tell them about what I do for my community and what I envision to see it through in my time of life."

So the cultural center, if it happens while I'm alive, that will be a good thing. But if happens when I'm not, I will still die happy and I will look down from the heavens and support the people who will be doing it in my absence.

Epilogue

As I finish this, it is 2021, and today is 6 years since I stayed back at Eshemuli and told Frances that he should open a medium-sized shop. This book covered three years of my journey. I thought I would do the first five years, but the momentum came to a stop, so here we are.

I included certain stories to paint a picture for you of what this has been like as I have navigated this incredible call to Kenya. Some of the stories were to show you the miracles I experienced, and some were to show you the opposition. I believe that both were necessary for me to do this work.

I've tried to be cautious with names and experiences, because my objective isn't to put people in a negative light. I honor their role in my journey, and I am grateful for the lessons I learned from them. If the journey seems confusing, that's because it has been. I often have experiences and then don't understand until much later how they served me.

Moses always tells me I am stronger than I realize, and most of the time he is right. This work has made me strong, because I've spent so much time on my knees in prayer.

There's another book in the near future, with additional stories and experiences that include the amazing people you have been able to meet so far. Some people who have read this book have asked questions about specific people and what happened to them. You'll just have to wait and see!

100 people. I have my answer to that question, now. I've actually taken more than 200 people to Kenya since we started expeditions in 2016. Perhaps that is why I stopped at this point. Perhaps what you need to get YOUR Kenya started is the starting point.

It takes faith. Rock solid, unshakeable, fall-to- your-knees every-day faith. That's what it takes.

Just know that I am cheering you on, because the world has problems that only you can solve with the gifts God has given you. I really believe that!

I'd love to invite you on a virtual expedition. Just opt-in at **www.100humanitarians.com** and watch it with your family. We hosted the virtual expedition on July 12, 2020 for our 5th anniversary.

Do you want to go to Kenya?

Acknowledgements

I could not do this work without the support of my family, both in the U.S. and Kenya. I love them very much.

Dave – Thank you for never telling me that I'm insane to do this work (at least not out loud!) Thank you for giving me blessings at a moment's notice when I'm freaking out.

Josh – Thank you for understanding when Kenya takes me away from you, and especially for holding my hand when I cry and telling me to keep going.

Clara – Thank you for being my partner in adventure, and for loving Kenya the way I do. I'm grateful we get to do this together.

Mom – Thank you for listening to my ramblings, editing my books, writing donation checks, and embracing Kenya as our family legacy.

Dad – Thank you for messaging me daily with "Dad Jokes" and insisting that Dave text you the moment I land so you know I'm safe.

Moses – Thank you for everything. None of this would have happened without you and your amazing leadership.

David – Thank you for making me promise to return to Kenya. Let's do a million trips.

Christine – Thank you for being my dada and setting an example for me of strength and resilience in the most challenging of circumstances.

Anita – Thank you for your patience, persistence, and love.

To the rest of my family and friends who have supported me in this journey, asante sana. I'm so grateful you are my village.

About the Author

Heidi Totten

Heidi Totten is an eclectic wife and mother of two relatively normal children. She spent her early career building technical teams around the world during the dot com era, and ten years ago launched her own business helping entrepreneurs and small businesses build their online presence. Her focus is connection and collaboration, and her personal business motto is "Content is king, but community builds the kingdom."

She is the best-selling author of *Homeschool on Fire: Be the CEO of Your Business and Homeschool* and *Success Through Failing*, a collaboration of 25 authors, including Christine and Anita from Kenya.

Heidi has helped hundreds of entrepreneurs over the past 3 years. She runs Heidi Totten Consulting (**www.heiditotten.com**) and is a founding partner with **The Promise Institute**. In her spare time, she is the Executive Director of 100 Humanitarians International, (**www.100humanitarians.com**) a grassroots non-profit that focuses on mentoring families in economic development in Kenya, Africa. She has taken over 200 people on 18 expeditions so far.

Her happy place is hauling down roads in Kenya in dusty jeeps, but she is also known for her love of tacos, guacamole, and chocolate.

Testimonials

Do you want to go to Kenya? Or anywhere in the world for that matter. I highly recommend reading My Maasai Name is Nemparnat, by Heidi Totten. A memoir of Heidi's courage to step out of her comfort zone. Her faith to follow her heart. Her resilience to rise above opposition and her passion to fulfill a dream. I can't wait to read the sequel. Thank you, Heidi, for sharing your life-changing experiences with us.

Becky Mackintosh
Expedition Leader

100 humanitarians does amazing work! I have been fortunate enough to go to Kenya twice and help with sustainable projects. I absolutely love this organization! – *Renae*

I have had the privilege of going to Kenya four times with 100 Humanitarians. I love that 100 Humanitarians is going deep and really making an impact in the communities they serve. To go back and be welcomed "home" by these people who accept you as their own. Serving along side them building GardenSaCs, training centers, teaching sewing and thermal cooking skills. Amazing. - *Cindy*

Truly Amazing!!

I was so very blessed to have the opportunity to go to Kenya with them earlier this year and was truly humbled not only by Heidi and the entire organization but by the amazing people in Kenya!! Thank you David and Moses and the group I was able to serve with!! All those involved and the volunteers for each expedition are amazing and bring life changing experiences to all involved. I have some health issues and was worried about slowing them down and didn't want to be a burden but was told that I was not to worry about it and that they would love to have me on their team. Although, I am sure that they served me more than I served them I am grateful for the opportunity I was given to go, serve and bless those around me! Thank you all for the amazing opportunity and yes.... can't wait to go again! I love serving as a volunteer and would love to serve on their board someday as they are truly making a difference in the world. – *Lori*

Our 16 year old daughter went to Kenya with Heidi and 100 humanitarians. She still talks about it and the life changing impact is it had on her. We love the mission and the passion with 100 humanitarian. We will be sending her again! - *Cristie*

My husband and I went to Kenya with 100 Humanitarians this year and we are amazed at the way they served the people of Bomet and the Masai Mara. We not only built garden boxes but taught the people how to do so to become self sufficient. We also took part in building a training/mentoring center next to the sewing center. We set up a water project on the Mara. We taught and mentored the young men and young women students in a secondary school and at a girls shelter leaving many "Days for

Girls" kits so the young girls can stay in school during their time of the month and continue their education. Definitely a worthy cause. All proceeds we donated went to the people we served and projects we worked on. I would totally go again! A life changing experience! – *Pam*

I have been extremely blessed to have 100 Humanitarians introduced to me. I went on the March 2019 trip and was blown away at the service opportunities 100 H is providing to the good people of Kenya. I will continue to seek to participate and support 100 H in any way I can and look forward to the opportunity to return to Kenya and serve my friends and family again.

Allen Roberds
Board Chair

What 100 Humanitarians international is doing in Kenya is truly remarkable! Creating an economical community where there has not been one is no small feat! Educating the families of the Maasai to garden and sew and work together in a new age is an amazing undertaking! I've met the lead of their team In Kenya and when in his presence hearing him speak of the changes that have occurred touches my heart at the deepest levels. Heidi Totten has amazingly created a nonprofit organization that teaches these tribes to be self reliant and that there are people who care about what happens in their lives! I cannot wait to join the team on an expedition! To be a part of something this important is a lifelong dream!! – *Robyn Scott*

I've been to Kenya five times now and I can't wait to go back later this year! From teaching skills to building garden towers and training centers together to make and impact, 100 Humanitarians has it right. I have been changed for the better from my experiences. Kenya has my heart, the people are amazing and welcoming. I've learned so much from them. If you have the chance, come be part of this wonderful organization.

Marissa Waldrop
Programs Director

My daughters and I just returned from our expedition with 100 Humanitarians a week ago and will be forever changed from the experience. We're already talking about when we can go back! What I love about this organization is that they truly create self reliance within the communities they work with. It really is about giving them a "hand up" rather than just a hand out. I can't wait to see the continued progress in upcoming expeditions. I also can't say enough how much we appreciated their team IN Kenya. Christine, Anita, Moses, David, John, and David...all of whom made the experience even much more special as they shared personal stories, taught us about their culture and saw to our safety and comfort. ♡ - **_Millie_**

I took my family to work with this incredible organization just a couple weeks ago. Their connection with the community, their ability to have everyone actively participate, the culture.... everything was incredible. I worked hard, saw incredible sights, cried and built new friendships. My daughter's (ages 8 and almost 10) were inspired and loved the experience as much as I did. We plan on volunteering next year as well. – *Lynn*

I've fallen in love with the work we do in Kenya. On both trips of which I've been a part, I've witnessed the pure love of spirit touching spirit. When we donated a cow to one lady, the entire village came out to greet us with a song of thanks that we could hear a quarter mile away. You can't imagine what an incredibly life-altering experience that is! On the other trip, we built fences for garden areas to keep out livestock (think chickens and goats) and let the plants thrive. And thrive they did!

Oh yes ... and safari. Never a bad thing. :) Please, won't you join us? – *Chris*

I have been to Kenya twice with 100 Humanitarians. This last trip I took my 11 year old daughter with me. I will never be able to properly explain how being involved in these projects have help my life and the life of my family. I can only hope that what I have contributed has helped an ounce of what I have received. My heart will never be there same. I have also made life long friends and connections...which in my opinion is the most important part of Humanitarian work...the people!!! - *Melodee*

I was told that I would go to Kenya to serve the people there but would soon discover that Kenya would serve me and my 13 year old son. That was exactly what happened. I laughed, cried, and loved the Kenyan people. We helped them to build garden boxes, build fences and assisted them in creating sustainable resources that would help them year after year. I love the fact that this organization doesn't simply give a hand out but gives a hand up instead. Helping the Kenyan people feel empowered to help themselves fosters a sense of independence and success-which is what the people want. These beautiful people love with their whole heart. They want to improve their situations and allow future generations a better life. – **Wendy**

Taking my two boys to Kenya was one of the best things I've ever done. When the thought first popped in my mind, I brushed it aside, thinking there was no way. We had too much going on, we couldn't afford it, it would be better to wait. However, for some reason I kept feeling this pull and I finally decided I knew I had to do it. I didn't know why or how, but I knew I had to. I followed my intuition and the universe took care of the rest. There are no words to describe and do it justice. The land, the people, the service, the gratitude, and the love is greater than anything I've ever experienced. It opens your heart, healing you and all those around you. The only way to change our lives, is to change our heart. My boys were able to experience this early enough in their lives that they will forever be changed because of it. In a lot of ways we were stagnant before we left, but we all came home ready to accomplish whatever the universe brings our way. I don't know when or how, but I know I will be going back to Kenya again. – **Holly**

I went to Kenya with 100 Humanitarians just a few weeks ago and took my 11 year old daughter. Not only did it give her confidence I have not seen in her in years, but she made lifelong friends and saw what it was really like to serve and make an impact. It will be the first of many trips for me becuase of the impact these beautiful people have had on me and the impact and relationship I want to continue to have with them. There is such much good that this organization is doing. On our trip we did projects in Bomet painting a learning center and planting trees along side the local people. We visited a Girls Rescue Center, and taught them how to make their own underwear from used tshirts. We went to a school and taught and gave out Days for Girls kits and played with the children. We went to the Maasai village and spent time learning from their culture and building relationships and playing with the children. We built a fence for Mama Helen and saw how beautifully she improved on the gardens she was given weeks before. We built several tower gardens, planted more trees, and threw seed balls to establish more families, schools, and organizations.

You go to Kenya to serve, and you leave Kenya with pieces of your heart left behind and a new outlook on life and the things that really matter. I can't wait to go again! - *Jentrey*